Jordan's Point, Virginia

Archaeology in Perspective, Prehistoric to Modern Times

Martha W. McCartney

ISBN - 978-0-615-45540-2

Virginia Department of Historic Resources
2801 Kensington Avenue
Richmond, Virginia 23221

www.dhr.virginia.gov

Distributed by the University of Virginia Press

http://www.upress.virginia.edu/

ACKNOWLEDGMENTS

Many individuals, organizations, and institutions contributed illustrations, original artwork, editing, or layout and all around support for this project. Their enthusiasm and support for this work is greatly appreciated. Those include Paris Ashton, Creative Director, Office of Graphic Communications, at Virginia's Department of General Services; the book's designer Judith Rumble; Bobbie Hair Grainger and Dan Hawks of the Jamestown-Yorktown Foundation; Marianne Martin, Barbara Lombardi, Ywone Edwards-Ingram, and Andrew Edwards of the Colonial Williamsburg Foundation; Jessica Suess of The Bodleian Library, Oxford University; David Riggs and Melanie Pereira of the National Park Service; Beverley Straube of Preservation Virginia; Nicholas Luccketti of the James River Institute for Archaeology; Dr. Virginia Cherry, Library Director, Richard Bland College; artist Ed Hatch for permission to reproduce his painting of the Jordan's Point Lighthouse; Jamie May for artifact illustrations; Jefferson Collins, Curator, Agecroft Hall; Claudia Jew and Jeanne Willoz-Egnor of the Mariner's Museum; John Kolbe of The Library of Virginia; Dick Hoffeditz and John Quarstein of the Virginia War Museum; and Taft Kiser of Cultural Resources Inc. At the Virginia Department of Historic Resources, special thanks to Randall B. Jones and David K. Hazzard, and to others who assisted in this publication: Kathleen S. Kilpatrick, Catherine Slusser, Mike Barber, Jennifer Mayton, Quatro Hubbard, and Lisa Williams. And last, but certainly not least, thanks to the numerous archaeologists whose tireless work at Jordan's Point preserved critically important information about Virginia's past.

Contents

If there is "a world in a grain of sand," as the poet William Blake writes, then imagine what archaeology can reveal at a richly layered triangle of land known as Jordan's Point, situated along the James River, just down river from the City of Hopewell. What archaeologists discovered there through careful investigations sponsored by the Virginia Department of Historic Resources and conducted during the closing decades of the last century is a path into the worlds of Virginia prehistory, colonial, and post-colonial history. The story of those worlds runs from the site's long occupation by Virginia's First People (Early Archaic through Late Woodland into the early Contact era) to its association with many of Virginia's First Families (most notably the Blands), and its evolution through the Civil War and into the 20th century.

As this book reveals, the archaeological data produced is simply remarkable and underscores the site's importance to our understanding of Native American prehistory, of the clash of Indian and European cultures during the Contact-era, of colonial settlement, and of a planter's life through the 18th and early 19th-centuries, when Jordan's Point was the home to generations of the Bland family. Among the findings, archaeologists discovered the presence of a large and dispersed Native American settlement, with evidence of 35 structures (the most recorded anywhere in Virginia), an ossuary, and copper beads and other grave goods. Additionally, the site yielded one of the best collections of European 17th-century artifacts in North America, as well as much information about the multi-generational evolution of the Bland plantation.

Today Jordan's Point contains a modern subdivision, "Jordan on the James." What made it possible for archaeologists to investigate the site, prior to its development as a housing complex, is Virginia's powerful Threatened Sites program administered by the Virginia Department of Historic Resources. Although little known to the general public, this program has been responsible for ground-breaking archaeological research at a diversity of significant sites throughout the Commonwealth since the program's inception in 1986. In terms of yield, however, the work at Jordan's Point remains among the most important completed under the Threatened Sites program for the extent and significance of the information and the artifacts recovered there.

With this concise and well-illustrated book, author and research historian Martha W. McCartney adds to her already formidable contributions to our knowledge as she relates the history of Jordan's Point. She weaves together an array of primary and secondary sources and archaeological reports to provide the reader with a keen understanding of Virginia's deep cultural roots and history as she chronicles the evolution of this site, named for its first European settler, Samuel Jordan, who acquired the point in 1621. In so doing, McCartney offers us a series of worlds, all contained within this little promontory along the James River. Anyone interested in Virginia history will want Martha McCartney's book in his or her library.

Kathleen S. Kilpatrick
Director, Virginia Department of Historic Resources, 2011

Jordan's Point, an almost triangular promontory that protrudes from the James River's lower bank, is situated in Prince George County, just east of where the James and Appomattox Rivers converge. A broad, elevated terrace that overlooks the James, Jordan's Point is bound by small streams, tidal marshes and protective uplands that soar to a height of 100 feet or more. The cultural features that archaeologists have unearthed at Jordan's Point document changes in human history that span literally thousands of years.

In 1607 when the first European colonists saw Jordan's Point, it was graced by the houses and cleared fields of natives they would call the Weyanoke. Virginia colonist Samuel Jordan established a community called Jordan's Journey around 1621, giving his name to what became known as Jordan's Point. In time, the settlement became a hub of social and political life.

By 1660, Jordan's Point had come into possession of the Blands, one of England's most important mercantile families. They leased their property to one or more of their agents, usually merchants and mariners involved in inter-colonial trade. Richard Bland I and his descendants developed Jordan's Point into a family seat and working plantation they retained until after the Civil War. At Jordan's Point enslaved men, women, and children toiled in the fields, enabling the Blands to prosper. Richard Bland IV went on to become a distinguished American patriot and one of his sons became a physician.

Fortunately for modern generations, many of the cultural features at Jordan's Point survived beneath the surface of the soil until archaeologists had an opportunity to examine them. Undoubtedly some important prehistoric and historic resources have been lost forever or await accidental discovery.

THE HISTORY OF ARCHAEOLOGY AT JORDAN'S POINT

Jordan's Point has been a known source of prehistoric Indian relics since at least the 1930s. Collections from the site were included in Dr. Clifford Evans' important study of Virginia prehistory, *A Ceramic Study of Virginia Archaeology*, published in 1955. During the 1960s Colonel Howard A. MacCord conducted salvage excavations in an area adjacent to State Route 156 that was to be disturbed by road construction. The aboriginal cultural materials he unearthed were at a location now designated 44PG1 in the state's inventory of archaeological sites. It was the first archaeological site registered in Prince George County. During the 1970s E. Randolph Turner III, a doctoral candidate, surveyed Jordan's Point and concluded that it was one of the most impressive prehistoric sites in eastern Virginia.

During the early 1980s archaeologists from Virginia Commonwealth University (VCU) visited Jordan's Point, then the site of the Hopewell Airport, and noted that fragments of seventeenth century ceramic vessels, tobacco pipes, and other early-dated artifacts were present. Private collectors reported discovering sixteenth century German jettons, possible evidence of early seventeenth century occupation. VCU student Ralph Porter, a member of the Archeological Society of Virginia (ASV), conducted a systematic surface study of Jordan's Point and created a map documenting many of the promontory's archaeological resources.

Rumors that the Hopewell Airport was being sold to a land developer sparked the Virginia Department of Historic Resources' (VDHR) interest in Jordan's Point. This led to the funding of a series of archaeological and historical studies that were undertaken by various individuals and institutions. A six-fold increase in the 1988 General Assembly funding of the Threatened Sites program allowed archaeological data to be recovered from Jordan's Point. Nine Late Woodland Indian house patterns were uncovered at 44PG303 prior to road construction. Artifacts retrieved from several early seventeenth century historic sites at Jordan's Point included large metal objects such as pieces of armor, that were found to be in unusually good condition. All of the objects recovered from Jordan's Point have been catalogued and preserved by VDHR curators, making them available for study and exhibition.

During 1987 and 1988 archaeologists from the James River Institute for Archaeology (JRIA), conducted excavations under the auspices of the VDHR and the Association for the Preservation of Virginia Antiquities (APVA, now Preservation Virginia), with contributions made by the Lower James River Association and the James River Corporation. JRIA personnel investigated six archaeological sites at Jordan's Point, notably 44PG151, 44PG200, 44PG302, 440G303, 44PG315, and 44PG333. They elaborated upon VCU's work at 44PG151, 44PG302, and 44PG303, but presented new data on 44PG300, 44PG315, and 44PG333.

Salvage excavations were undertaken at 44PG300 by James G. Harrison III, a volunteer, who produced a detailed report. Human burials were excavated at 44PG302, 33PG315, and 44PG333 by Charles and Mary Ellen Hodges, and at

44PG303 by Garrett Fesler. Donna and Clifford Boyd of Radford University and Dr. Douglas Owsley of the Smithsonian Institution analyzed the human remains unearthed at 44PG300, 44PG315, and 44PG302. Around the same time JRIA archaeologists were working at Jordan's Point, the author conducted extensive archival research and developed a property history that enabled Jordan's Point's cultural features to be placed within an appropriate historical context.

During 1990 and 1991 archaeological excavations were undertaken at Jordan's Point by VCU's Archaeological Research Center personnel who focused their attention upon 44PG302. The primary purpose of their work, which was underwritten by VDHR's Threatened Sites Program, a grant from the National Geographic Society, and private funding, was rescuing important archaeological information and cultural materials that were threatened with destruction by residential development. Archaeological field school students from VCU and from the ASV's field school assisted with excavations as did volunteers from the Greater Richmond Chapter of the ASV and others who generously gave of their time. Technical assistance was provided by personnel from the Colonial Williamsburg Foundation, the National Museum of Natural History, and the JRIA.

During the 1990 field season, VCU archaeologists focused their attention upon the southeast quadrant of 44PG302. They unearthed the remains of several Native American houses, a possible ceremonial fire pit, and several very early colonial buildings. They also examined Native American and colonial burials. In 1991 the enclosed colonial settlement at 44PG302 was exposed and mapped and a larger portion of the site was studied. Afterward, artifacts were processed and catalogued.

In 1991 cultural features at Jordan's Point were discovered by archaeologist David K. Hazzard of the VDHR within an area that was to be developed. At the site designated 44PG307, he identified a large seventeenth century borrow pit, a series of early eighteenth century root cellars, and two early seventeenth century refuse deposits.

During 1992 and 1993 when VCU archaeologists conducted excavations at 44PG307, they examined a total of eighteen structures, some of which probably were Native American features associated with the Indian village present at Jordan's Point prior to European occupation. Seven of the historic period structures examined at 44PG307 were found to date to the early seventeenth century, whereas three other structures appear to have been associated with the late seventeenth and early eighteenth centuries. During the 1992-1993 field season, VCU archaeologists also studied a building that was associated with 44PG151. They surmised that it was a dwelling that had been occupied by a moderately comfortable household that had an abundance of material goods but lacked luxuries. They concluded that the structure may have belonged to one of the Bland family's farm managers or perhaps to an artisan.

When time and funding permitted, JRIA curator Beverley Straube and VCU curator Taft Kiser analyzed artifacts recovered from Jordan's Point and Dr. Joanne Bowen of the Colonial Williamsburg Foundation analyzed faunal remains. Separately and collectively, their studies have added immensely to what we know about Jordan's Point's lengthy history of human occupation.

In October 2005 the Frances Bland Randolph Chapter of the National Society Daughters of the American Revolution hosted the dedication of a Virginia Historical Marker honoring the patriot Richard Bland II. At that ceremony the DAR gravesite marker honoring Richard Bland IV was rededicated and the gravesite of Richard Bland II was designated a Literary Landmark by the Friends of U.S.A. and the Friends of the Richard Bland College Library.

Today, Jordan's Point is home to a development known as Jordan on the James and all evidence of its archaeological riches has faded from view. Thanks to VDHR's Threatened Sites program, much important information has been preserved that otherwise would have been lost.

Martha W. McCartney

The manner of their attire and painting them Selves when they goe to their generall huntings or at theire Solomne feasts.

Their Manner of Dressing. The Jamestown-Yorktown Collection, Williamsburg, Va. USA.

CHAPTER 1

Virginia's Native People

Thousands of years before the first European colonists arrived in Virginia, an indigenous population inhabited the coastal plain, leaving a faint imprint upon the land. The early history of the Indians or Native Americans, though largely unrecorded, is an integral part of America's heritage. Our knowledge of these people comes to us through archaeology.

THE PALEOINDIANS (15,000 TO 8000 BC)

Between 15,000 and 8000 BC, when the Paleoindians lived, the climate and environment were vastly different than they are now, for enormous continental glaciers were a controlling factor. The sea level was much lower than it is today and the Chesapeake Bay was just a narrow river. Winters were long and hard and summers were short, cool, and moist. Streams flowed through tundra-like grasslands and forests of spruce, pine and fir covered most of Virginia at that time. Large portions of the continental shelf were exposed that currently are underwater and many of today's slow-moving rivers were much more active.

The first people, the Paleoindians, lived in small, mobile groups called bands that anthropologists liken to an extended family. They roamed across a large but somewhat limited area, establishing small, temporary encampments where food was available. They derived much of their nourishment from plants, small game and fish, and meat from large mammals like deer, elk, bear, and moose. Hunters developed stone tools that enabled them to kill animals that were attracted to rivers, lakes and salt licks.

THE EARLY ARCHAIC PERIOD (8000 TO 6000 BC)

During the Early Archaic period, significant environmental changes occurred, for the cold, moist climate of the Pleistocene Age changed to a more temperate, dryer one. Warmer winds melted the glaciers hundreds of miles to the north of present-day Virginia and the ocean's temperature rose. A rise in sea level spread water across the coastal plain. It created the Chesapeake Bay and covered or eroded most of the places frequented by the very early hunters. Forests of pine and oak replaced open grasslands. Elk, deer, and bear were abundant and readily available to hunters. As vegetation became more profuse, Early Archaic people gathered more plant foods such as fruits and nuts. As nomadic hunter-gatherers, they made abundant use of animal skins, especially those of deer. They also began to vary the size and shape of their stone tools, making side or corner notches that were used to attach points to spears. During the Early Archaic period, the population grew, thanks to a more hospitable environment.

THE MIDDLE ARCHAIC PERIOD (6000 TO 2500 BC)

By the time the Middle Archaic period arrived, Virginia's Indians had adjusted well to their new environment and long winters and short summers had been replaced by seasons much as we have today. Large amounts of rain forced rivers to overflow their banks, depositing rich topsoil on the floodplain. The Indians went about their hunting and gathering, in accord with the seasons, and tools and weapons became more functional and sophisticated. Women began using mortars and pestles to crush nuts and seeds from which they could prepare food. Using their stone axes, Middle Archaic people cut wood they used to build houses and make fires. Game animals became more accessible, making hunting easier.

THE LATE ARCHAIC PERIOD (2500 TO 1200 BC)

During the Late Archaic period, there were perhaps tens of thousands of Indians in Virginia. Because the floodplain, which was forested, contained an abundance of plant and animal life, Late Archaic period Indians enjoyed a wide variety of foods, greatly enhancing their diet. The floodplain attracted small bands of people, who merged to form small settlements or hamlets. Native people also began learning how to nurture certain plant species. Some commenced raising varieties of gourds and squash, and they began to store crops for leaner times, placing food stuffs in storage pits in or near their homes. The transition from foraging to collecting gave rise to the establishment of substantial, perhaps semi-sedentary, base camps along major streams, where fish and shellfish could be gathered. In the coastal plain, saltwater oysters became an important food source. The Indians' discarded oyster shells formed middens or refuse heaps. When excavating Late Archaic sites, archaeologists have found the remains of dogs, the Indians' only domesticated animal.

THE EARLY WOODLAND PERIOD (1200 TO 500 BC)

The Woodland period embraces the more sedentary Native cultures that lived in the woodlands of the eastern United States. Although the pattern of subsistence varied little in the Late Archaic and the Early Woodland periods, a major innovation occurred. During the Early Woodland period, Native people began making and firing clay vessels for cooking and storage. First, they dug good clay from a riverbank or bluff and blended it with water. They added crushed rock or shell, for they had learned through experience that these additives (tempering) reduced shrinking and cracking during drying and firing. The clay pot, once fabricated by hand, was allowed to air dry. Then it was baked in an open fire. Once cooled, the Indians had a vessel that could be used for cooking or storage. Archaeologists use differences in the size, shape, body, surface treatment, and decoration of clay vessels to assign dates to sites that Woodland period natives occupied.

THE MIDDLE WOODLAND PERIOD (500 BC TO AD 900)

As the population grew, the diverse groups who lived in scattered but settled hamlets made the transition from bands to tribal-level organization. Subsistence patterns began to evolve and eventually culminated in sedentary horticultural practices. Middle Woodland people planted corn, a domesticated plant that was brought into the eastern United States from Mexico. The introduction of corn, in combination with better nutrition, enabled the population to increase during this period. Archaeologists believe that religious ceremonies linked to the harvesting and planting of corn may have led to the development of societies in which rank and status were important. The natives began using the bow and arrow as a hunting weapon instead of spears. Middle Woodland period people experimented with specialized crafts and increased their trading activities. This enabled Native leaders to spread their cultural traditions and beliefs and share their knowledge of farming.

LATE WOODLAND PERIOD (900 TO 1600 AD)

By the Late Woodland period, Tidewater Virginia Indians, though more sedentary than their forebears, followed a seasonal pattern of hunting and gathering. They lived along the banks of tidal waterways during the warm months and in winter, when their gardens were dormant and fishing was less productive, they moved into the interior and relied upon stored food and whatever game they could procure. Therefore it was a relatively mobile existence. Coastal Virginia's natives lived in large villages that included hundreds, perhaps thousands, of people. Their relatively substantial houses usually were built upon the floodplain or low-lying necks of land that had rich, sandy soil. The Indians' houses were clustered close together or interspersed with fields used for gardens. Sometimes villages were surrounded by a palisade. Late Woodland villages were organized around a complex economic, social, and political structure. Village life provided residents with social contacts, security, and an opportunity to accumulate wealth. Ceremonial life was important and creativity flourished. The Indians fabricated a wide variety of pottery forms and wrought objects of stone, copper and shell that reflected their belief system.

Projectile points found at archeological site 44PG302. VDHR photo.

The axe changed shape over time. Top: an early axe, notched and chipped from stone, 5000 BC. Middle: grooved axe, 3000 BC. Bottom: celt, AD 1500, flaked, pecked, and then smoothed with sand. VDHR photo.

The Indians typically grew maize, beans, and squash during the spring and summer months and as time went on, they began growing tobacco. Women and elderly men usually planted crops, employing the slash-and-burn method of clearing the ground they used for agriculture. The vegetable crops the Indians grew helped to fulfill their nutritional needs. This allowed them to stay in one location for longer periods of time. Improved nutrition enabled Late Woodland people to thrive and become more populous. Waterways were viewed as a source of food and a conduit of transportation. Sometimes, if a stream were narrow, the natives would build their towns on both sides. Their houses usually were located close to the shore and sometimes the town extended along the waterfront for a considerable distance.

Archaeologists believe that control of the food supply led to the development of Native societies with differences in the rank or status of certain individuals. In chiefdoms, which had begun to develop by the late 1500s, leaders accepted tribute, which they retained or redistributed. In time, the literally hundreds of villages that existed in Tidewater Virginia began to compete for territory and economic supremacy. Weaker tribes were forced to pay tribute to stronger ones that guaranteed them protection in times of war. By the mid-to-late sixteenth century a paramount chiefdom began to emerge. Virginia's Algonquians shared a common linguistic bond with some of the Native peoples to the north and south, a distinct dialect that set them apart from those communicating in the Iroquoian, Siouan and other tongues. By the time the first colonists arrived, the Indians' way of life was well established.

PRELUDE TO COLONIZATION

Virginia Indians in the coastal plain probably encountered their first Europeans around 1525 and offered them food and fresh water, the hospitality they traditionally extended to strangers. The natives suffered from the experience, for Spanish and Portuguese raided their villages, seizing captives. In 1570, a small group of Spanish Jesuits hoped to establish a mission in coastal Virginia, intending to use a captured—and converted—Indian youth as an intermediary in spreading their message. The Jesuits' attempts went awry and their deaths were avenged by the commander of Cuba's governor who arrived in 1572. The Spaniards then weighed anchor, undoubtedly leaving in their wake a legacy of dread and suspicion. In 1585 some of the Roanoke colonists made an exploratory visit to the south side of Hampton Roads and found some of the natives hospitable.

The Towne of Secota, an engraving by Theodor de Bry. The Jamestown-Yorktown Collection, Williamsburg, Va. USA.

In 1607, when the English established a permanent settlement on Jamestown Island, Tidewater Virginia's natives were under the sway of Wahunsonacock or Powhatan, a paramount chief. He reigned over thirty-two districts that encompassed more than 150 villages, whose inhabitants paid him tribute and supported him in times of war. Captain John Smith described Powhatan as a monarch to whom many lesser kings (or werowances) were subservient. Thus, the people of the Powhatan Chiefdom were members of a society in which rank and status were important.

Scholars believe that the Powhatan Chiefdom took form during the 1570s, when Powhatan inherited the right to lead six or more small chiefdoms within a vast territory that extended from the falls of the James River, northward to the

York. When the first colonists arrived, Powhatan was trying to seize control of the Chickahominy, a strong Native group governed by a council of eight elders, not a solitary, all-powerful leader. He also attempted to assert his supremacy over some of the lesser chiefdoms between the Rappahannock and Potomac Rivers. By the close of the following year Powhatan controlled almost all of the subchiefdoms or districts located in Virginia's coastal plain.

Early explorers, who recorded their observations, shed light upon how Virginia's Native inhabitants lived. However, it is important to remember that those narratives merely reflect the writers' perception of Native culture. Their sketches and written accounts capture a sense of Indian life, but the more subtle differences between the two cultural groups surely escaped notice. It is likely that they also misunderstood or misinterpreted larger issues.

AN INVITING SETTING

Jordan's Point is a triangular-shaped land form that juts northward into the James River some ten to twenty-five feet above the river. This terrace is covered with Pamunkey sandy loam that would have been moderately fertile and would have produced excellent harvests of corn. Jordan's Point's base is backed by two creeks and uplands that rise dramatically. These uplands, which would have been forested when the natives were making use of Jordan's Point, would have been excellent foraging territory. Nearby waterways would have been a good source of tuckahoe and other plants useful to Native people and shad and herring would have been abundant in the spring.

The Way they Broyle their Fish, an engraving by Theodor de Bry. The Jamestown-Yorktown Collection, Williamsburg, Va. USA.

ARCHAEOLOGY AND JORDAN'S POINT'S FIRST PEOPLE

Jordan's Point has been a known source of prehistoric Indian relics since at least the 1930s. Colonel Howard A. MacCord visited Jordan's Point in 1939 and excavated a small pit that was exposed in the embankment of the road leading to the Hopewell-Charles City Ferry. He found numerous fragments of shell-tempered, fabric-impressed pottery and a dog skeleton. Later, the site was among those studied by Clifford Evans and C. G. Holland. Evans observed that pot sherds and projectile points were scattered along the James River's shoreline. When he viewed Jordan's Point from the air, he saw large, dark circular patterns in the soil, which he surmised were Indian camp sites or house patterns.

In 1965 Colonel MacCord returned to Jordan's Point and collected cultural material from an area that was to be disturbed by the improvement of State Route 156. He identified several types of projectile points and four types of Native pottery, attributing the majority to the pre-ceramic or Archaic Period. With the assistance of volunteers, he delved into the soil, excavating a strip that paralleled the highway. Seventeen cultural features were found, including several aboriginal trash or storage pits, three circular pits, and five stone hearths. Also unearthed were human burials. The location at which MacCord worked was designated 44PG1 in the state's inventory of archaeological sites.

When archaeologists from VCU conducted excavations at Jordan's Point during the early 1990s, they found limited amounts of Archaic and Early Woodland materials and surmised that the area had been the site of a substantial Indian settlement. Prehistoric occupation is believed to date back seven to eight thousand years and there is good evidence for the presence of the Savannah River complex people.

OTHER NATIVE SITES AT JORDAN'S POINT

Excavations at Jordan's Point, conducted by archaeologists from VCU and the JRIA, identified portions of a large, internally-dispersed Indian village dating from the Late Woodland to the early Contact period and included as many as fourteen houses. These cultural features corresponded to the location of the aboriginal settlement Captain John Smith showed on his well known map of Virginia. The irregular pattern in which the buildings were arranged may reflect their association with family gardens and planting fields, the type of dispersed villages William Strachey described in 1612 as being "without forme of street, far and wyde asunder."

Features associated with the Indian settlement at Jordan's Point were found at the sites designated 44PG151, 44PG300, 44PG302, 44PG303, and 44PG307, and at an isolated ossuary (44PG333). Houses were identified at all but two of these sites (44PG151 and 44PG333), perhaps because they lacked ready access to potable water. Archaeologists found considerable variation in the types of Native American structures they unearthed at Jordan's Point. Some of those differences may have been temporal, but it is more likely that they were functional.

In all, at least thirty-five Native American structures, mostly houses, have been identified at Jordan's Point. They range in size from a round structure that measured only fifteen feet in diameter to a much larger oval structure (near 44PG302 and 44PG303) that measured thirty feet in length. One oblong structure had a flattened end. Any internal hearths that may have once existed have been destroyed by plowing. Archaeologists concluded that most of the Native houses at Jordan's Point were oriented so that they would deflect the cold winter wind. Each house usually had a door near a corner of the long axis. Some buildings had upright posts inside a door, perhaps to support a mat that served as a windbreak or privacy screen.

The discovery of Gaston and Roanoke pottery types at Jordan's Point suggests that Late Woodland occupation was intense during its earlier phase. Sherds of Townsend and other fabric-impressed wares made up the majority of the Native ceramics found during the earlier portion of the Late Woodland period. Plain/smoothed hard-fired wares tempered with shell, sand, or quartz and typically seen in the Late Woodland period, were in use around the time Native occupation ended at Jordan's Point. The lithics found at Jordan's Point were non-diagnostic and mainly consisted of quartzite flakes, and to a lesser extent, quartz. Rhyolite and greenstone flakes were found in small quantities.

The Native features archaeologists unearthed at Jordan's Point have the potential to illuminate the relationship between the James River social groups that formed the core of Powhatan's chiefdom and the Siouan and Occaneechee speaking groups to the south. At Jordan's Point was found a distinctly communal area containing possible granaries, an Okee circle, and burials. They have the potential to shed light upon Powhatan community structure.

44PG300

When archaeologists from JRIA investigated the Native American features Jay Harrison previously identified and designated 44PG300, they found six complete dwellings, four incomplete buildings, and traces of ten additional structures. Archaeological salvage work at 44PG300 revealed that Native American structures extended inland 360 feet from the shoreline of Jordan's Point's east side, spanning a distance of at least one hundred feet. Most of these Native houses were oblong and oriented so that they could deflect the wintry winds and strong gusts that tend to follow the James River. In summer, the mats covering the buildings' walls could be rolled up, so that cooling breezes could pass through.

44PG302

At 44PG302, archaeologists discovered evidence of Native occupation dating to the late prehistoric-early protohistoric period. During the 1990 and 1991 excavation seasons, a total of eight Native American houses were identified and examined, along with another building that had been partially destroyed by plowing. Most of these structures were oval and probably were constructed of green saplings set into the ground. Their opposing ends would have been bent over to form domed or arbor-like roofs. Sapling cross-pieces would have been lashed to vertical members and exposed surfaces would have been covered with marsh grass mats or bark. Some of the Native buildings found at 44PG302 had squared-off ends or were rounded and probably had interior posts. They may have been covered with daub (mud mixed with vegetation) and had specialized uses or they may date to a somewhat earlier period. Any hearths that were present would have been shallow and therefore probably were destroyed by deep plowing while Jordan's Point was used for farming. During the 1580s artist and scientist John White produced detailed watercolor renderings of Indian houses similar to those found at 44PG302.

A large oval building (Structure 22) that measured twenty-five feet long and seventeen and a half feet wide was found at 44PG302. Sherds of Roanoke Simple Stamped pottery were recovered from the site as was a fragment of shell-tempered plain/smoothed ware. Structure 2, a large, oval wigwam-style building, was found beneath early colonial fortifications and probably was a dwelling. A second large wigwam-style building (Structure 3, a probable dwelling) was found nearby. When a small patch of ground was cleared at 44PG302, just west of an area containing colonial burials, a possible ceremonial fire pit was discovered, as was a Native American burial. When acreage at the western periphery of 44PG302 was cleared and examined, four additional Native American structures were found, Structures 9, 11, 12, and 13. Feature 417, a large rectangular cavity with straight sides and a flat bottom, may have been a burial pit. It was surrounded by a ring of posts that may have formed a circular enclosure. On the other hand, John White's drawings suggest that Feature 417 may have been a dance circle or a special area used for feasting and socializing. Unfortunately, construction of a domestic complex during the 1620s intruded upon some of the prehistoric and protohistoric features at 44PG302.

Controlled surface collections at 44PG302 yielded large amounts of Native American lithic debris and fire-cracked rocks, along with sparsely scattered ceramics that included simple stamped and fabric-impressed sherds. The predominant type of ceramics at 44PG302 was Gaston Simple Stamped, concentrated in the vicinity of the Native American buildings on the site. These ceramics' inclusion in colonial fill documents the repetitive use of 44PG302.

Projectile points recovered from 44PG302 by avocational and professional archaeologists range from Early Archaic through Late Woodland or protohistoric, with a heavy representation of Savannah River and Middle Archaic types. Among the tools found at 44PG302 were a bifacial knife, a grooved axe, a bifacial drill, scrapers, and cobble tools that may have been used as grinding- or hammer-stones. Debitage included flakes, cores, and chunks.

44PG303

Archaeologists from VCU found evidence of Native American occupation at 44PG303 immediately prior to the construction of a road to a modern housing development. Present were the remains of at least nine Late Woodland houses that were clustered and varied in shape. These houses ranged in size from eighteen to thirty feet in length and thirteen to seventeen feet in width. Some of the structures overlapped and were not present at the same time. House types ranged from oval to rounded and would have been structurally sturdier than the flat-ended houses John White depicted in drawings that date to the 1580s. However, some of the Native buildings at Jordan's point were large and had squared-off corners, giving them an elongated, rectangular form. Gaston Simple Stamped and Roanoke ware, associated with the protohistoric and Contact periods in Virginia, ca. 1500 to 1620, dominated the Native ceramics collected at 44PG303. Although relatively few artifacts were present at 44PG303, perhaps because of extensive ground disturbance, the Indian houses found there probably were associated with the dispersed village that was at Jordan's Point during the Late Woodland period. One cluster of buildings may have served as a village center.

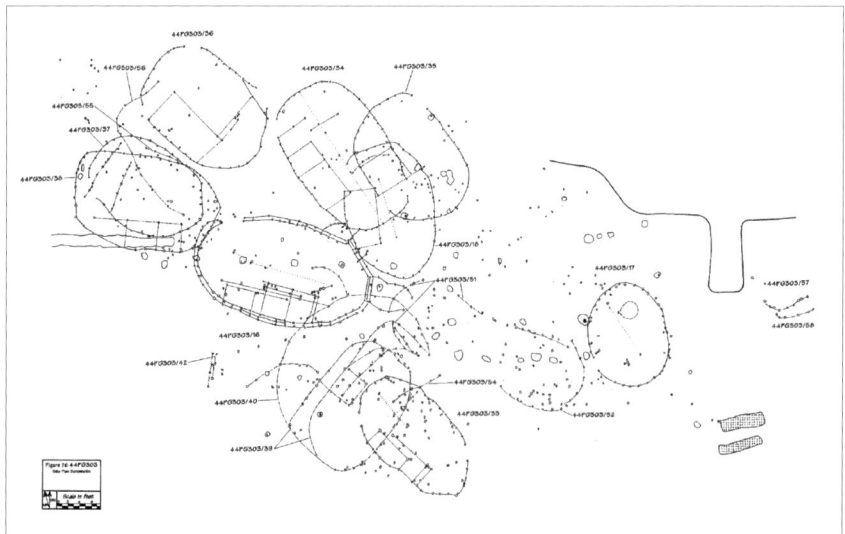

Cultural features associated with Native American occupancy at 44PG303. Courtesy Virginia Company Foundation.

One unusually large building (Structure 16) measured thirty-and-a-half-feet long and ten-feet wide and may have belonged to a chief. It was elaborately constructed with support posts that were larger and more closely spaced than other houses and its wall posts were set in pairs. The main door, which was four-feet wide, was in the east end of the building and was sheltered by a six-foot-long vestibule. Inside the house was archaeological evidence of a long built-in bench or shelf. Multiple lines of post holes leading away from the entrance door suggest that the building may have had post-supported partitions.

44PG307

At 44PG307, typical oval house forms were found. One complex consisted of at least three overlapping or rebuilt houses.

INDIAN GRAVES

Burials were found to the east-southeast of 44PG307 and at 44PG315. A dog burial found in association with 44PG307, part of the dispersed Indian village, contained Gaston Simple Stamped pottery, which suggests that the animal was interred during the Late Woodland period. Nearby, at 44PG151, a human burial was found that contained the remains of a small dog. Although dog burials occur in abundance elsewhere within the Weyanoke Indians' territory, the interment of a woman and a dog (perhaps a companion animal) may be unique. One Native man interred at Jordan's Point was buried in an extended position. He was wearing a leather band to which copper was attached. Copper beads also were found in his grave site. Another man, who was buried in a fully flexed position, was interred with sheet copper that formed a band across his throat, probably a necklace made of copper and leather. Copper beads also were found near the man's pelvis and shoulder and he may have had copper ear ornaments. This individual probably was of high status in the Native community.

One individual interred at Jordan's Point suggests a blending of Native and European cultures. Because bone preservation was very poor, the gender and ethnicity of this person is uncertain. Although Late Woodland artifacts were present, the decedent had been laid out in the style of a Christian burial.

An ossuary exposed by heavy equipment used during the course of development was designated 44PG333. Although partially destroyed before it was examined by archaeologists, it contained nine human skulls arranged in a semi-circle. This ossuary may have been associated with 44PG1, which predated the occupation associated with 44PG151, 300, 302, 303, and 307. Dr. Donna C. Boyd of Radford University determined that the human remains in the ossuary at 44PG333 represented a minimum of seventeen individuals. The gender of only twelve of these Native people could be determined: seven adults and five youths or children. Many of the bones in the ossuary bore cuts and grooves that prob-

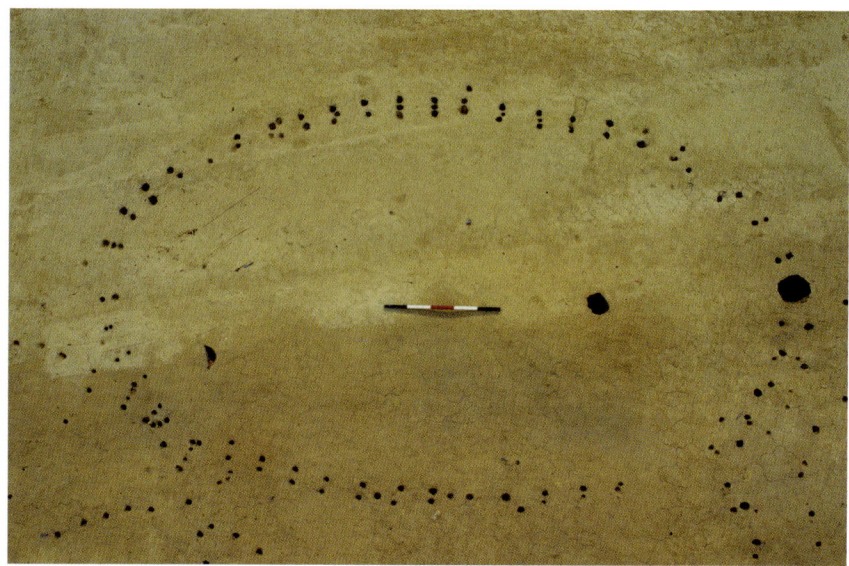

An overhead view of one of more than thirty Native American oval house footprints that survived and archaeologists exposed below the plowed fields at Jordan's Point. The pole in the middle of the picture is five-feet long, so the house is roughly 17 by 30 feet. The dwelling, like the colonial-era one depicted on the opposite page (bottom), was an earthfast *building, meaning its structural supports were anchored in the ground. VDHR photo.*

ably were attributable to impact by modern construction. However, in three instances the cuts and grooves appeared to be ancient. This raises the possibility that the marks were inflicted by de-fleshing, which was a very common practice among natives.

Four Native American burials, which were in a poor state of preservation, were identified and carefully excavated at 44PG302. All of these single interments were adult men and women. Two burials were extended, one was flexed, and the fourth probably was a bundle burial. One man, who probably was age forty or older, is believed to have been associated with the protohistoric village that was present around the time the first European colonists arrived. His grave contained sherds of Gaston Simple Stamped pottery. Only the flexed burial is believed to predate the protohistoric Indian village.

A remarkable variety of burial practices existed at Jordan's Point. They included primary burials of solitary individuals in extended or flexed positions, apparent secondary interments of single individuals, and multiple second burials in ossuaries. As few grave goods were found, it is likely that many were perishable items. The burials showing the greatest variety appear to have been associated with later Native occupation of Jordan's Point. This trend seems to have been associated with the coastal plain as a whole and may be linked to the rise of the Powhatan Chiefdom.

Excavations at Jordan's Point: (a) Cross section of an early seventeenth-century saw pit; an abundance of deer bone is situated on the unexcavated back half of the pit. Courtesy of VCU; (b) An archaeologist working at 44PG151; note wine bottles in situ on a tiled floor in a brick cellar. VDHR photo; (c) Three turn of the seventeenth-eighteenth-century broad hoes, found in a root cellar at 44PG307. Photo by David K. Hazzard; (d) A breast plate and helmet recovered from an early seventeenth-century trash pit at site 44PG300. Photo by J.G. Harrison, III; (e) A partially excavated late seventeenth-early eighteenth century earthfast building at 44PG151; note rectangular root cellars within the building's footprint and the burnt clay on right side of photo, indicating location of a chimney. Courtesy of James River Institute for Archaeology.

The Jamestown-Yorktown Collection, Williamsburg, Va. USA.

CHAPTER 2

Cultures Collide

THE FIRST COLONISTS

On Saturday, December 20, 1606, three small ships, the *Susan Constant*, the *Discovery* and the *Godspeed*, set sail from London catching the outbound tide. Encountering favorable winds, they headed out to sea on an adventure that changed the course of history. The fleet's commander, Captain Christopher Newport, had unrivaled experience in navigating the American coastline, whereas Bartholomew Gosnold and Gabriel Archer had been to New England and were familiar with the natives and their language. Several in the group were aware of the attempts to establish a colony on Roanoke Island and had some idea of what to expect, once they reached land. The survival skills of Captain John Smith, an experienced explorer and soldier of fortune, eventually proved invaluable. The ability of Captains Smith and Newport to communicate with the natives suggests that they had some knowledge of the Algonquian language.

During the newly arrived colonists' first days in Virginia, they sailed inland to explore the countryside. They went ashore from time to time and found magnificent timber and lush vegetation, fields covered with brilliantly colored flowers, an abundance of fruit and berries, fertile soil, a countryside teeming with wildfowl and game, and waters brimming with seafood. They also saw large meadows that would make excellent pasturage for cattle. One writer described Virginia as a veritable paradise on earth.

When the first colonists moved up the broad river called the Powhatan, later the James, they encountered natives whose bodies were ornamented

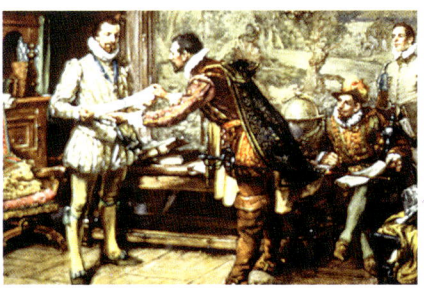

Sir Thomas Smith receiving charter from King James. Courtesy of the National Park Service, Colonial National Historical Park, Jamestown Collection.

with brightly colored furs and jewelry of bone, shell, and copper, and whose hair was adorned with feathers and animal horns. According to Captain John Smith, some of the Indians welcomed the newcomers hospitably, offering food and entertainment. Others discharged arrows and then fled from the colonists' retaliatory gunfire.

Smith commented that Indian men spent most of their time hunting, fishing, and engaging in wars, while the women and children made mats, baskets, and pottery and raised the crops upon which their villages depended. He described the Powhatans as generally tall and straight, with black hair and dusky complexions, and noted that the men rarely had beards. He said that the natives were exceptionally strong and agile and tolerated even the worst weather.

On May 13th Captain Christopher Newport's small fleet arrived at a marsh-rimmed peninsula that resembled an island. The river's channel ran so close to the shore that the colonists could moor their ships to the trees. The next day, they established an outpost called James Cittie or Jamestown, the first permanent English settlement in North America.

CRITICAL TIMING

The University of Arkansas's study of tree-ring data from a bald cypress near Jamestown Island reveals that the first European colonists arrived during a period of severe drought that lasted from 1606 to 1612, the driest period in 770 years. Conditions were particularly severe in Tidewater Virginia near Jamestown. Drought conditions would have created a crisis for natives and colonists alike, for plant materials would not have been readily available for subsistence. Also, water quality would have been at its poorest, perhaps affecting the supply of fish and game. Regional drought would have increased the salinity of the lower James River, especially in the oligohaline zone, the area in which the exchange between fresh and salt water in the river is minimal. Thus, when the first Virginia colonists arrived, the natives they encountered would have experienced a bad crop year and probably had food shortages.

EARLY EXPLORATION

Shortly after the first colonists began planting a settlement on Jamestown Island, Captain Christopher Newport and a party of explorers sailed up the James River, taking note of the Indian villages along the river banks. They would have seen the large aboriginal settlement located at Jordan's Point, to the west of Tar Bay. Captain John Smith's topographically sensitive map, which provides detailed coverage of Tidewater Virginia, suggests that the Weyanoke Indians' territory spanned both sides of the James River. Other Indian villages, which Smith attributed to the Weyanoke and Appomattock, were located both east and west of the Jordan's Point. Smith indicated that a chief's village was located at Great Weyanoke or Weyanoke Point, on the north side of the James River,

*Trading with the Powhatan Indians. Courtesy of the National Park Service,
Colonial National Historical Park, Jamestown Collection.*

*Indian settlements in the James River's upper reaches, including the one at Jordan's Point.
The Bodleian Library, University of Oxford, shelfmark (E) F6:54 (39), 1758, fols 13v-14r.*

and that an "ordinary" village was situated at Jordan's Point. A 1635 patent for acreage called "the Indian field," located near the mouth of what is now called Jenny Creek, suggests that native occupation was conspicuous.

UNDERSTANDING THE NATIVES' LANGUAGE

Although some of the first colonists had a rudimentary knowledge of the Algonquin language, interpreters were needed to facilitate communication. Thomas Savage, a young boy who came to Virginia in 1608, was given to Powhatan, and Namontack, an Indian youth, was handed over to the English so that he could learn their language. Savage lived with Powhatan for almost three years and in time became a skillful interpreter who frequently went on trading voyages. Other Indians, such as Pocahontas, Chanco, and Kempes, who gained a working knowledge of the English language, would have facilitated communication between the natives and colonists.

DIFFERENCES IN PERCEPTION

The first English colonists, transferring to the New World the Jacobean idea of property rights, did not understand native concepts of landholding. Captain John Smith observed that within Virginia Indian towns, land was allocated to households by a local leader who was subservient to the paramount chief. While the native mode of land distribution bore a remote resemblance to the English tradition that all realty was owned by the monarch, the Indians' seasonal pattern of subsistence and the subtle but purposeful shifting movement of their towns had no parallel in English culture. Moreover, the colonists' need to fulfill certain legal requirements when staking a claim to land would have been unfamiliar to the Indians. In fact, the Powhatans considered land merely a part of the earth, like the sky, water, and the air, and therefore open to all for subsistence. Thus, the European concept of owning land was completely foreign to them.

Portrait of Captain John Smith. Courtesy of the author.

Although both cultures viewed accumulated wealth as an emblem of social status, they had a much different concept of inheritance, for with the Powhatan, it passed through the female line rather than the male. For example, Powhatan's chiefdom could descend to his next oldest brother or the son of his eldest sister but not to his own children. In light of the vast differences between the two peoples and their mutual lack of understanding, they were destined to collide.

It took English officials nearly a half century to realize that the natives' foraging territory was vital to subsistence. On the other hand, the Indians probably wondered why the English expected to retain possession of their land in perpetuity, even though it appeared vacant. Moreover, they probably could not understand why seemingly "abandoned" acreage was not available to others. First in 1640 and then in 1649, Virginia's governing officials formally recognized native groups' need for land of their own.

ATTEMPTS AT RELIGIOUS CONVERSION

Richard Hakluyt and other proponents of colonization spoke fervently of the opportunity to bring the Christian faith to native people in the New World and the Virginia Company's first charter described the propagation of Christianity as a noble work. In fact, letters written by some of the first Anglican clergymen who came to Virginia reveal that they were filled with a missionary zeal. However, the two cultures had vastly different views of religion. The Powhatans, while open to the idea of a Christian deity, were reluctant to renounce their own gods. Some of the colony's early leaders spoke of bringing Christianity to the natives but they also were preoccupied with establishing control and typically employed force to impose their will. What's more, they took the natives' land whenever they wanted it and often seized their food supply.

DEPENDENCE UPON THE INDIANS

Eight or nine months after Captain Christopher Newport had departed from Virginia, the First Supply of new immigrants arrived, discovering that relatively few of the original colonists remained alive. A Second Supply of settlers arrived a few months later. Within two months they had consumed their store of food, after which time they were forced to disperse and live among the Indians. The Third Supply of new colonists set out for Virginia in May 1609 in a fleet of nine ships, but their vessels were scattered and blown off course during a hurricane. By August, seven of the ships arrived at Jamestown, carrying 300 famished passengers. During this period, when the colony was under a military form of government and its inhabitants lived communally, the settlers made their homes on Jamestown Island. They did, however, venture into the mainland to explore, trade with the Indians, and seek sustenance. The struggle to survive during the winter of 1609-1610 was so arduous that it was dubbed the Starving Time. However, the summer months also were challenging, for the settlers at Jamestown endured much sickness. Some early writers astutely observed that the countryside toward the head of the James River was a more healthful location.

In May 1610, Sir Thomas Gates and Sir George Somers, whose ship, the *Seaventure*, had been with the Third Supply but had been shipwrecked in the Bermuda Islands, arrived in the colony. Finding at Jamestown only a handful of sick and starving colonists, Gates resolved to take them to Newfoundland, where they could secure nourishment and passage back to England. Only the timely arrival of Lord De La Warr's three ships a month later, bearing both men and provisions, averted abandonment of the fledgling colony.

THE COLONY UNDER MARTIAL LAW

In May 1611 Sir Thomas Dale arrived in Virginia with 300 new settlers and provisions, supplies, livestock, and seeds to grow garden crops. Dale, a military man with extensive experience in the Netherlands, was appalled by the conditions he found. Rightly or wrongly, he attributed the colony's woes to a lack of strong leadership and within a month of his arrival instituted martial law. This harsh military code of justice included moral and religious rules and invoked the death penalty for even minor infractions of the law. Dale required the colonists to work toward their own support, but allowed them to reap the profits of their own labor, once they had fulfilled their communal responsibility. In time, many of the measures Dale adopted were termed inhumane and the cruelty of his administration became legendary. But when he left Virginia in May 1616, the colony was on a relatively sound footing and its survival was assured.

SEIZING NATIVE LAND

Sir Thomas Dale responded to the Virginia Company's orders to build the colony's principal town in a healthier, more defensible location by establishing several new settlements toward the head of the James River. Although two of the communities that Dale founded, Henricus and Coxendale, lay several miles above the Appomattox River, most of the new seats that he established lay downstream, in territory that later fell within the bounds of the Corporation of Charles City. These settlements included Bermuda City and Hundred, Digges Hundred, Upper Hundred (or Curles), Rochdale Hundred, and West and Shirley Hundred and Island, not far from Jordan's Point.

Dale and his men drove the Appomattox Indians from their habitation near the mouth of the river that still bears their name and by January 1614 he had established the New Bermudas or Bermuda Incorporation. According to Ralph Hamor, Dale's men built a two-mile-long palisade across the elongated peninsula that became known as Bermuda (Charles) Hundred, a promontory that extends from the west side of the Appomattox River's mouth. Hamor stated that Bermuda Hundred's settlers were seated along the riverfront and the palisade. According to John Rolfe, a resident of Bermuda Hundred, in 1614 the community was home to Sir Thomas Dale, Captain George Yeardley, and the Rev. Alexander Whitaker, a clergyman. Another individual who lived at Bermuda Hundred was Samuel Jordan, who around 1621 established a plantation called Jordan's Journey or Beggars Bush.

In 1616 Bermuda Hundred had 119 inhabitants, some of whom were engaged in making pitch and tar, potash, charcoal, and other useful commodities. By April 1619 the fortifications at Bermuda Hundred reportedly were weak and in disrepair. In March 1620 Bermuda Hundred was home to 123 men, 30 women, and 31 children. The population probably was inflated by refugees from Captain Christopher Lawne's Warresqueak plantation, who by November 1619 had withdrawn to Bermuda Hundred in hope of recovering their health. By 1620 some parcels in Bermuda Hundred had been assigned to individual landowners. One was Jordan's Journey founder Samuel Jordan, who had a fifty-acre tract on the riverfront that contained a house and another small parcel that also was developed.

Pocahontas and John Rolfe married in April 1614. Courtesy of the National Park Service, Colonial National Historical Park, Jamestown Collection.

CRITICAL CHANGES

Sir Thomas Dale introduced several innovative policies that were designed to encourage the colonists to become self-supporting and he opened the colony to Dutch trade. He also dealt with the Indians from a position of strength. John Rolfe's April 1614 marriage to Powhatan's daughter, Pocahontas, ushered in several years of peace, during which the Virginia colonists gained a firmer footing and the tobacco economy literally took root.

Although many of the communities that Sir Thomas Dale established were abandoned soon after his departure from Virginia in 1616, some hard-won but invaluable lessons had been learned. One was that the settlers were capable of producing their own food supply. Another was that the colony's success depended upon its inhabitants' being allowed to exercise personal initiative. Fortunately, the opportunity to reap substantial profits from growing tobacco, a highly marketable commodity, coincided with several major changes in governmental policy, particularly with regard to land ownership. These factors combined to fuel the spread of settlement and they attracted new immigrants and investors—to the Indians' detriment.

AGRICULTURE: THE KEY TO SUCCESS

During Sir Thomas Dale's administration John Rolfe conducted his famous tobacco experiments, learning how to grow a palatable and marketable strain of "the weed." Tobacco quickly became such a lucrative money crop that it attained acceptance as currency.

All farmers had to defend their own settlements and the colony, perform thirty-one days public service a year, provide their own households with food and clothing, and contribute two and a half barrels of Indian corn per male household member to the common store. No one could plant tobacco until he had put in two acres of corn per male household member. Once that basic obligation was fulfilled, the colonists could raise as much tobacco as they wished.

In time, Virginia Company officials learned that the colony critically needed farmers and laborers to produce a dependable and adequate food supply and women to establish homes. The "hard way of living" one early writer described was not a lifestyle to which gentlemen and urbanites could readily adapt, even willingly. Many colonists planted tobacco instead of food crops and then complained about hunger while awaiting supplies from England. They also bartered with the Indians for corn and other food and sometimes took it by force, making enemies in the process. John Pory in 1619 declared that Virginia was ideal for agriculture, but he admitted that the colony's riches lay in tobacco. The boom in tobacco prices continued until around 1630, when overproduction glutted the market.

THE NATIVES' LOSS OF TERRITORY

Powhatan died in 1618, a year after the death of his daughter, Pocahontas. His brother and long-term successor as paramount chief, Opechancanough, presented Captain George Yeardley with a large tract of land on the north side of the James River. The roughly triangular peninsula, known as Tanks (Tanx or Little) Weyanoke, encompassed 2,200 acres. Documentary sources suggest that Yeardley seated some of his people at Weyanoke before he had secured the Virginia Company's official approval, which came in 1618. The Virginia Company also assigned Yeardley 1,000 acres on the lower side of the James at Tobacco Point, where he established the plantation called Flowerdew Hundred. Shortly after Governor George Yeardley's April 1619 arrival in Virginia, he placed some of his indentured servants at Weyanoke.

Overleaf:
In 1612, a published pamphlet titled "Virginia Discovered and Discribed [sic] by Captain John Smith" featured Smith's map of Virginia. Scholars at the Library of Virginia consider it "the most accurate and detailed map of the Chesapeake Bay and the Atlantic coastline produced in Europe until 1673." The map's geographical accuracy is remarkable, especially considering how quickly Smith, a Virginia Company investor, surveyed the area during his 1608-1609 voyages of exploration. As the Captain John Smith Chesapeake National Historic Trail website notes, "Smith's map records not only the geographic features of the Chesapeake, but also its cultural aspects, including more than 200 Indian towns. Many of the place names remain in use today." Many versions and derivatives of Smith's original map were published over the years. The one reproduced here, a color rendition that is extremely rare, is preserved at Oxford University and was among the "curiosities" that John Tradescant bequeathed to his friend, Elias Ashmole (1617-1692). In 1860, the Ashmolean Museum's collections were transferred to the Bodleian Library. ("Virginia Discovered and Discribed [sic] by Captain John Smith," 1612. Bodleian Library, Oxford University, MS Ashmole 1758 folio 14r.)

POWHATAN

Held this state & fashion when Capt. Smith
was deliuered to him prisoner

POWHATAN

MONACANS

MANN

P O W H A T A N

MARGOAGS

CHAWONS

Monahassanugh
Rassweck
Menafukapanough
Mastmacack
Mowhemcho
Stegara
Shackaconia

The Fales
Powhatan
Cattachiptico
Pafsaunkack
Uttrusfank
Arrohatteck
Orapaks
Appamatuck
Mysbuckpaffo
Accequeck
Seobeck
Nechanicek
Quackcohowaon
Martoughquaunk
Anafkenoans
Wighcocomoco
Massaw
Attamuck
Accoffumck
Muttamuffinfack
Sacobeck
Quackehowaon
Cheapsywe
Afsuettha
Pifpascoe
Kerahocak
Pifseseck

Jamestowne

Warraskoyack
Mathomauk
Mokete
Kiskiack
Werowcomoco
Opifcaramk
Chefapeack

Cape Henry
Cape Charles

Smyths Iles

Accomack
Keales

Wighcocomoco

KUSKA

Cape Comfort
Point Comfort

THE

VIRGINIAN SEA

Maſſaw- *Maſſawomeck* Omecks

RGINIA

14

The Saſque- ſahanougs are a Gyant like peo- ple thus a- tyred

Vechowis

N

Pamacoeack
Tauxenent
Namaſſingaakent
Aſſaomeck
Namorauahquend
Tamatuk
Nameus
Nuetchtanck
Pamacom
Quactataugh

BAY

Powels Iſle

Boxes poynt

Ozinies

Poynt Reſnac

Tockwogh fin:

TOCK
WOGHS

Cepewia

Attauck

Quadroque

Smiths fales
Saſquiſahanough
Saſquiſahanough fin:

Jeſiruck

SASQVE
HAN
OVGH

ATQV

Atquanachuke

ANACC

Tergeroyt mount

HVKES

and holfe

Leagues

Chickahokin

Macocks

10 17

Deſcribed by Captayn John Smith
by William Hole

John Rolfe and Tobacco. The Jamestown-Yorktown Collection, Williamsburg, Va. USA.

CHAPTER 3

The Colony Takes Root

THE VIRGINIA COMPANY'S GREAT CHARTER

In November 1618 the Virginia Company ratified its so-called Great Charter and a year later, Sir Edwin Sandys and his supporters wrested control from the company's merchant-investors. This led to the abandonment of martial law under which the colonists had languished for nine years. The Virginia Company's Great Charter paved the way for some sweeping changes, one of which was the introduction of a land policy that enabled colonists to own real estate and to work for personal gain. This, then, was the genesis of America's free enterprise system. Another important change was the establishment of representative government and a judicial system akin to local English law.

THE LINK BETWEEN LAND AND LABOR

One of the most important features of the Virginia Company's Great Charter became known as the headright system. It provided prospective immigrants with an incentive to leave overcrowded England and seek their fortunes in Virginia. But it also encouraged wealthy investors to underwrite much of the expense of colonization, for groups of investors could outfit and transport prospective colonists, on whose behalf they would acquire land and establish private or "particular" plantations. The opportunity to reap substantial profits from growing tobacco while accumulating land fueled the spread of settlement.

Under the headright system, so-called ancient planters (those who immigrated to Virginia at their own expense and lived there for at least three years prior to Sir Thomas Dale's May 1616 departure) were entitled to 100 acres of land. Those who came later, paid the cost of their own passage, and stayed in the colony for three years, were entitled to fifty acres of land. Anyone who underwrote the cost of another's transportation became eligible for fifty acres on his or her behalf. Thus, successful planters, by importing hired workers for their plantations, could fulfill their need for labor while amassing additional land.

Harvesting tobacco. Courtesy of the National Park Service, Colonial National Historical Park, Jamestown Collection.

Many people owned two or more tracts and circulated among them. Investors in Virginia Company stock were entitled to 100 acres per share and became eligible for a like amount when their first allotment was planted.

An indentured servant (or a minor's guardian) usually signed a contract with an agent, agreeing to exchange a certain number of years' work for transportation to Virginia. When the agent arrived in the colony, he sold the servant's contract, usually to a planter who wanted more hands to work his land. On the other hand, servants could be "ordered" from agents in the Mother Country. In the beginning, many of Virginia's indentured servants were members of the English middle class. These men and women, often in their teens and twenties, represented a broad cross-section of society. They included yeoman farmers, husbandmen, artisans, and laborers, but also some jailbirds and children. At first, males outnumbered females six to one, but eventually the sex ratio became somewhat more balanced.

Those who acquired indentured servants were supposed to provide them with food, clothing and shelter and could exact labor under certain conditions, exercising what the law deemed reasonable discipline. Indentured servants who became field hands usually toiled from dawn to dusk, six days a week, during the growing season. Adults usually served for four years, whereas those under fifteen sometimes were bound for seven or more years. Literate servants or those with special skills sometimes could negotiate for shorter terms. Servants who fulfilled the terms of their contracts were supposed to receive their "freedom dues," usually a quantity of corn and clothing. Former servants often leased land until they could acquire acreage of their own. New immigrants did likewise while fulfilling the headright system's residency requirements.

Virginia planters, when initially establishing homesteads, typically constructed and occupied crude huts while erecting weatherproof but insubstantial frame houses. Building a simple dwelling or "Virginia house" enabled patentees to legitimatize their land claims while fulfilling the need for basic shelter. Renting land to tenants and providing shelter to servants also encouraged the proliferation of impermanent housing.

THE NASCENCE OF REPRESENTATIVE GOVERNMENT

Although Virginia's governor and his council of state were chosen by Virginia Company officials, provisions were made for the colony to have a general assembly with burgesses elected by popular vote. It was the first such body of its kind to convene upon North American soil. When incoming governor, Sir George Yeardley, arrived at Jamestown on April 19, 1619, to assume the reins of government, he saw that the colony was subdivided into four corporations or boroughs. Each was vast in size and spanned both sides of the James River. Each settlement within those corporations was invited to send delegates or burgesses to Jamestown to convene in an assembly.

On July 30, 1619, the members of America's first legislative assembly gathered in the church at Jamestown. Present were Governor Yeardley, his six councilors, and two burgesses from almost all of the colony's settlements. Samuel Jordan was one of the two delegates representing Bermuda Hundred. After an opening prayer, the assembly's speaker, John Pory, read aloud excerpts from the Virginia Company's Great Charter and reviewed two of the four books of laws that had been sent to the colony. Then, the burgesses formed two committees to study the remaining books of laws. They had no right to challenge the rules set down for governing the colony, but could recommend changes they thought necessary.

First legislative assembly. Courtesy of the National Park Service, Colonial National Historical Park, Jamestown Collection.

Afterward, the burgesses drafted some laws that were subject to the monarch's approval. Laws were enacted against idleness, gambling, drunkenness and "excess in apparel," as well as against theft, murder and other criminal offenses. Indian trade was to be regulated by the colony's governing officials and only a limited number of natives were allowed to live within the settled territory. The colonists were required to provide their households with a year's supply of corn (or maize), storing some for use in times of need, and to plant vineyards, mulberry trees, and silk flax. Tobacco growers had to follow certain procedures when preparing their crop for market. No one was allowed to venture further than twenty miles from home, visit Indian towns, or undertake a voyage longer than seven days without obtaining permission from the governing officials.

Taking Slaves to Market. Courtesy of the Colonial Williamsburg Foundation, Department of Archaeological Research.

Ministers were to make note of all of the christenings, marriages and burials they performed, and household heads had to furnish the secretary of the colony with a list of those under their care. The clergy were to report to the authorities anyone suspected of committing moral offenses such as intoxication, fornication, or swearing. Thus, the link between church and state was tightly forged while Virginia had an Established Church. Captain John Smith reported that by 1622 courts had been set up "in convenient places," perhaps a reference to the right of private plantations' leaders to arbitrate disputes among their own people. At Jamestown the governor and his council convened regularly as a court. By 1625 there were local courts in two of the colony's corporations and one on the Eastern Shore.

THE FIRST BLACK IMMIGRANTS

In August 1619 an event occurred that forever changed the course of Virginia history. It was then that a Dutch frigate, fresh from a plundering expedition in the West Indies, sailed into Hampton Roads bearing twenty-some blacks. At Old Point Comfort the vessel's captain exchanged his black captives for some provisions he needed. Shortly thereafter, the newly arrived men and women were brought up to Jamestown and sold into servitude. A ship called the *Treasurer* left at least one African in Virginia shortly after the Dutch frigate's departure. Researchers now believe that these men and women came from Angola and that some had been converted to Christianity. Although the concept of institutionalized slavery did not arise until much later, Africans' distinctive appearance, unfamiliar language, and exotic cultural background set them apart from the other colonists and placed them at a decided disadvantage.

It is impossible to imagine the pain, anguish, humiliation, and brutality that Africans endured when they were captured, branded, and transported from their homeland. According to surviving accounts, African kings who lived in the interior of the continent sometimes had their agents ensnare other blacks, who were sold to slavers. These captives, tied together by the neck with leather thongs, were marched overland to the seacoast. There, they were sold to traders and then imprisoned and branded with the mark of the slaver who bought them. Next, they were loaded aboard the ships that brought them to the New World. During the "Middle Passage" from West Africa to America, shipboard conditions were cramped and unsanitary, producing an alarming death rate. Some captives were so distraught that they jumped overboard, committing suicide. It has been estimated that only half of the Africans captured and sold to slavers ever lived to reach the New World.

FUELING GROWTH AND DEVELOPMENT

One of Governor George Yeardley's first tasks was setting aside special tracts of land intended to reap profits for Company investors and to support high ranking officials and the clergy. By 1620 all of those parcels had been laid out. In March 1620, there were 892 European colonists living in Virginia, with males outnumbering females by nearly seven to one. Also present were thirty-

Arrival of the Young Women at Jamestown, Harper's Monthly Magazine, April 1883. Courtesy of the National Park Service, Colonial National Historical Park, Jamestown Collection.

Planting a settlement. Courtesy of the National Park Service, Colonial National Historical Park, Jamestown Collection.

two blacks (seventeen women and fifteen men) and four Indians, who like the blacks, were said to be "in ye service of severall planters." None of the men and women listed in the March 1620 census were said to be living at Jordan's Journey. In 1620 the Virginia colonists had a relatively ample supply of livestock (cattle, horses, goats, and tame swine) and military equipment, and more than 220 "habitable houses," not counting barns and storehouses.

The colony's population was highly mobile, as new immigrants arrived constantly and groups of investors continued to underwrite the cost of establishing privately sponsored plantations. By the mid-1620s the Virginia colony was so firmly entrenched that few doubted it would survive. The settlers had demonstrated that they could produce their own food supply and it was acknowledged that farmers and skilled workers were critical to the colony's well-being. The headright system enticed would-be colonists to seek their fortunes in Virginia, whereas the opportunity to reap substantial profits from growing tobacco, a highly marketable commodity, served to fuel the spread of settlement. Despite the Natives' objections, the colonists were here to stay.

Virginians began claiming property to which they were entitled under the headright system and servants, upon fulfilling their terms of indenture, began acquiring land of their own. Meanwhile, established planters acquired increasing amounts of acreage by bringing servants to the colony. Many individuals who possessed land in two or more locations placed tenants on their properties. The establishment of these widely scattered plantations not only impinged upon vast amounts of Native territory, it also made the colonists vulnerable to assault.

THE NATIVES STRIKE BACK

Despite the years of peace that followed Pocahontas' marriage to John Rolfe, after her death in 1617 and that of her father, Powhatan, the following year, a more militant attitude emerged on the part of the natives, who were led by the charismatic paramount chief, Opechancanough. On Friday, March 22, 1622, the warriors of the Powhatan Chiefdom, threatened by the inroads of expanding settlement, launched a carefully orchestrated attack upon the sparsely inhabited plantations along the James River. It was a desperate attempt to drive the colonists from their soil. At the end of the day nearly 350 men, women and children lay dead, somewhat more than a third of the colonists. Contemporary accounts reveal that the Indians entered the homes of the unsuspecting settlers and then fell upon them, sometimes mutilating their corpses. In the wake of the attack, the Indians returned to several outlying plantations and attempted to force their inhabitants to leave, and as soon as they did, put their homesteads to the torch. The governor declared martial law and ordered the occupants of remote plantations to abandon their homes. Jordan's Point and seven other settlements were strengthened and held, as were certain plantations on the lower side of the James River, across from Jamestown Island. Each was entrusted to a commander, whose power was absolute in matters of war.

Then, the colonists began making retaliatory raids upon the Indians' villages, burning their houses and destroying their food supplies. Virginia Company officials, though sympathetic to the colonists' plight, blamed them for settling so

The March 22, 1622, Indian attack. Courtesy of the National Park Service, Colonial National Historical Park, Jamestown Collection.

far apart that they could not unite for mutual defense. Yet despite this criticism, they insisted that it was essential for the colonists to reoccupy their plantations. In the end, it was probably the common knowledge that abandoned land quickly grows up in underbrush that impelled the planters to return to their homesteads.

Although the natives did what they could to resist the colonists' attacks, by early April 1623 they were suffering. It was then that the paramount chief Opechancanough, though his emissaries, made an overture for peace. He sent word that there had been enough bloodshed and that his people were starving because the colonists were destroying their food supply. Opechancanough offered to return some English captives and to allow the colonists to plant in peace, if his people could do the same. The governor and council, though distrustful, agreed to a truce they admittedly intended to break. The Indians, meanwhile, exchanged their nineteen female prisoners for some glass beads. Captain William Tucker, a veteran of the Dale years, and Dr. John Pott, the colony's physician-general, gained notoriety by attempting to kill some Indian leaders by toasting a spurious peace treaty with a cup of poisonous wine.

Pikeman by Jacob de Gheyn, 1607.

Within months, the Virginia colonists' confidence grew and they began returning to their plantations, armed with outmoded military equipment Virginia Company officials obtained from the Tower of London. One man claimed that planters were obliged to work with a hoe in one hand and a gun or sword in the other. Retaliatory raids, undertaken from time to time, kept the Indians at bay. Memories of the 1622 Indian attack were kept alive by the natives' sporadic forays and March 22nd was declared a holy day that was to be commemorated with prayer and fasting. The colonists were ordered to build palisades around their dwellings and those occupying necks of land were told to cordon them off with a line of posts and planks.

From 1624 on, local military commanders like William Farrar of Jordan's Point were supposed to see that their settlements' able bodied men were sufficiently armed and provided with powder and ammunition. A 1626 law required military commanders to muster their men on holidays, at which time they would drill them and inspect their weapons. Commanders were to make sure that their men's guns were in good repair and that their weaponry was complete.

By 1627 officials sent word to England that most colonists' houses were fortified against the Indians. However, a careful examination of the 1625 muster suggests that the colonists' palisaded houses rarely were classified as "forts." In fact, five plantations in the upper reaches of the James River were equipped with heavy ordnance, including three that had served as strongholds immediately after the 1622 attack, but none (including Jordan's Point) were said to have forts. It is perhaps significant that almost all the settlements to which heavy ordnance was attributed were home to "ancient planters," men who had come to Virginia prior to the 1616 departure of Sir Thomas Dale. Trade with the Indians was forbidden and it became an accepted stratagem to undertake campaigns against them in March (prior to planting, when food stores were minimal), in July (while crops were growing), and in November (after harvest and when loss of shelter would be most critical).

THE VIRGINIA COMPANY'S DEMISE

During the winter of 1622-1623 Bermuda's ex-governor visited Virginia. He dispatched a scathing account to England, claiming that new immigrants could be seen "dyinge under hedges and in the woods" where their corpses lay unburied for days. He said that the colony's ironworks were destroyed and its "Furnaces for Glass and Pots" were at a standstill. He added that Jamestown was unfortified and had only three pieces of ordnance for defense. Other critics alleged that Jamestown's wharf was in ruins and that goods put ashore were regularly inundated by the tide. One man even asserted that the colonists longed for a return to martial law. But those who had endured the rigors of Sir Thomas Dale's government insisted that his policies had yielded immense pain without substantive gain. Ultimately, internal politics and insuperable financial problems took their toll and in 1624 the Virginia Company's third and final charter was revoked. Although there were attempts to revive it, most colonists believed they would fare better under the Crown. By 1626 some of the Virginia Company's land had come into private hands and its indentured servants had been set free.

LIFE IN THE COLONY

Demographic records compiled during 1624 and 1625 reveal that by that time, family life was firmly rooted in Virginia. Many households consisted of a married couple and one or more children, often the offspring from one or both parents' prior marriages. Thus, step-siblings, half-siblings, and full blooded

The early settlers' houses were impermanent. Courtesy of the National Park Service, Colonial National Historical Park, Jamestown Collection.

relatives tended to progress with a parent or step-parent through a series of marriages almost always terminated by death. The accumulation of wealth through successive marriages and the hardships that were part of frontier life probably made widows and widowers eager to remarry. As the colony became better established, more women came to Virginia and the number of marriages and births rose.

MAINTAINING LAW AND ORDER

As the population increased and loosely defined communities developed, disagreements among neighbors sometimes ended up in court. Those living upon privately-sponsored plantations could seek justice from a local commander or leader, but others had to appear before the governor's council, which convened regularly as a court. There was an increased need for a local judiciary and by 1632, monthly courts were convening in five locations. Matters aired before the council ranged from offenses against religious laws (such as failing to pay church dues or hunting hogs on Sunday) to capital crimes such as murder and treason. Many of the punishments the council handed down during the 1620s and 30s today would be deemed barbaric. For example, a man's ears might be loped off for perjury or he might be whipped for a sex offense. But it was a brutal and bloody era in which corporal punishments such as hanging, maiming, and dismemberment were permissible under the law and belief in witchcraft, omens, apparitions, and other supernatural phenomena was common. Reputation and status were highly prized and successful planters could elevate their social standing rapidly by accumulating wealth.

Commerce and trade. Courtesy of the National Park Service, Colonial National Historical Park, Jamestown Collection.

When the governor's council (Council of State) convened as a Quarter Court decisions could be made that affected the colony as a whole. For example, in 1624 every male household head over the age of twenty was required to plant four mulberry trees and twenty vines and to enclose his garden. Each household also had to plant an adequate amount of corn. By the end of the decade, colonists had to plant two acres of corn "for every head that worketh the land" but no more than 2,000 tobacco plants per household member. No one could move from one plantation to another without official approval. All vessels entering Virginia waters had to pause at Jamestown before touching land elsewhere. This helped in the collection of import duties but it also allowed government officials (many of whom were merchants) first access to incoming ships' cargoes.

By 1628, Virginia authorities had begun trying to control the quality and quantity of the tobacco produced in the colony. Inspectors were to examine the tobacco to be shipped abroad and planters were ordered to set their plants at least four and a half feet apart, gathering only twelve leaves from each. Storage warehouses were built upon the riverbanks, where hogsheads of tobacco could be kept until loaded aboard an outbound ship. Virginians' dependence upon tobacco as their principal money crop created complex economic problems, with alternating "booms" and "busts" in the market. Even so, tobacco was many colonists' principal source of income.

RELATIONS WITH THE INDIANS

Despite the colonists' successive offensives, the natives continued to fight back and made isolated forays upon outlying settlements, especially in the upper reaches of the James. In the spring of 1626 a Weyanoke Indian came to Shirley Hundred, where he was captured and taken to officials in Jamestown. Later, he was taken to the Eastern Shore by Captain William Eppes. Tensions were high and in April 1627 the governor issued a warning that the Indians were expected to attack at any time. By August 1628 a formal peace agreement had been made, but government officials admitted they would honor it only until they saw a fit opportunity to break it. By January 1629 they had found the excuse they were looking for. The Indians were accused of killing the planters' hogs and cattle, stealing their hoes, and slaying men hunting in the woods. However, official records disclose that all formal treaties with the natives were declared extinct because the settlers had been remiss in maintaining their own defenses. Thus, the 1628 peace treaty was not broken because the Indians failed to abide by it, but because the colonists had failed to provide for their own defense.

THE COLONY IN 1629

In March 1629, each of the colony's loosely defined communities was assigned a military commander, who had to muster and drill his men. William Farrar was placed in command of the settlers at Jordan's Point. All households

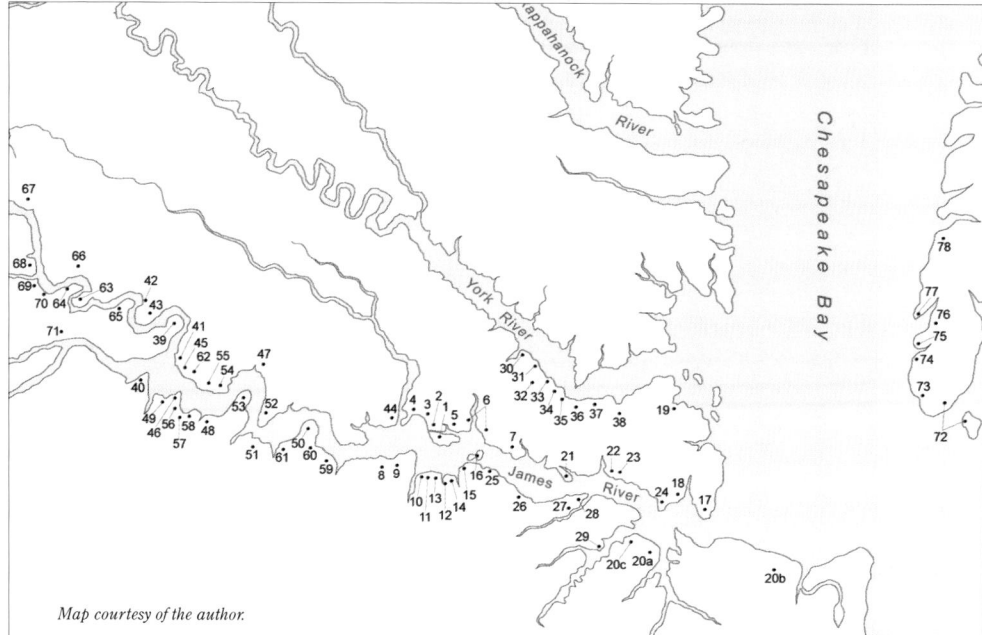

Map courtesy of the author.

1. Jamestown Island
2. Glasshouse
3. Governor's Land (The Maine and Pasbehay)
4. Company in James City
5. Neck O'Land
6. Archer's Hope
7. Martin's Hundred
8. Burrows Hill (Burrows Mount, Smith's Mount)
9. Paces Paines
10. Captain Roger Smith's Plantation
11. Treasurer's Plantation
12. Hugh Crowder's Plantation
13. William Ewen's Plantation
14. Captain William Powell's Plantation
15. Captain Samuel Mathew's Plantation
16. Hog Island
17. Old Point Comfort, the Company Land, and the Common Land in Elizabeth City
18. Elizabeth City (west side of the Hampton River)
19. Elizabeth City (near the mouth of the York River)
20. Elizabeth City (lower side of the James River)
   a. Elizabeth River
   b. Lynnhaven area
   c. Nansemond River
21. Mulberry Island
22. Blunt Point and Stanley Hundred
23. Mathews Manor (Denbigh)

24. Newportes News (Marie's Mount)
25. Captain Christopher Lawne's Plantation
26. Bennett's Welcome (Warresqueak)
27. Basses Choice
28. Giles Jones's Plantation at Day's Point
29. Nansemond
30. King's Creek Plantation
31. Ringfield
32. The Indian Field Plantation
33. Francis Morgan's Plantation
34. William Prior's Plantation
35. Richard Townsend's Plantation
36. Maritiau's Plantation
37. York Plantation
38. Wormeley Creek
39. Bermuda Hundred (Charles Hundred, the Nether Hundred, Neck of Land in Charles City)
40. Bermuda City (Charles City)
41. West and Shirley Hundred and West and Shirley Hundred Island
42. Upper Hundred (Curles)
43. Digges Hundred
44. Smith's or Smyth's (Southampton) Hundred
45. Causey's Care (Cleare)
46. Jordan's Journey (Beggars Bush)
47. Swinehowe's Plantation
48. Maycock's (Macock's) Plantation
49. Captain John Woodlief's Plantation
50. Powle-Brooke or Merchants Hope
51. Captain Henry Spellman's Dividend

52. Weyanoke (Tanks or Tanx Weyanoke)
53. Flowerdew (Peirsey's) Hundred
54. Westover
55. Berkeley Hundred
56. Chaplin's Choice
57. William Bikar's Plantation
58. Truelove's Plantation
59. Captain John Martin's Plantation (Martin's Brandon)
60. Captain John Bargrave's Plantation
61. Captain John Ward's Plantation
62. Company Land in Charles City
63. City of Henrico (Henricus Island)
64. Coxendale
65. Rochdale (Roxdale) Hundred, Rock Hall
66. College Land and Arrohattock (Sir Thomas Smith's Hundred)
67. The Falls (West Fork, Nonsuch)
68. Falling Creek
69. Thomas Sheffield's Plantation
70. John and Alice Proctor's Plantation
71. Peirsey's Plantation (Peirsey's Toile)
72. Smith's Island, Golden Quarter (Dale's Gift)
73. Old Plantation Creek
74. Captain William Eppes's Plantation
75. Secretary's Plantation
76. Company Land
77. Savages Neck
78. Sir George Yeardley's Plantation

were ordered to assemble for daily prayer and every plantation was required to have a special place in which worship services could be held. The colonists were forbidden to waste powder by firing weapons during times of celebration, and they could not venture out alone or unarmed. The colony's governing officials reiterated their order that all houses were to be enclosed by palisades.

When Captain John Smith described conditions in Virginia in 1629, he based his comments upon the testimony of several colonists, who were visiting England. One was Nathaniel Causey, then a resident of Jordan's Journey. Smith said that the settlers living along the James River seldom encountered any Indians, although their fires could be seen distantly in the woods. Colonists foolish enough to venture out alone and unarmed might be slain, but those whose plantations were defended by palisades had few worries about an Indian attack. Captain William Peirce, a council member, added that each plantation had armed men or musketeers who were prepared to fend off an Indian assault.

*An autumn harvest. Courtesy of the National Park Service,
Colonial National Historical Park, Jamestown Collection.*

CHAPTER 4

Jordan's Journey

THE PROGENITOR, SAMUEL JORDAN

Samuel Jordan (Jordain, Jorden, Jerden), who planted a settlement at Jordan's Point in 1621-1622, came to Virginia in 1610. He probably was aboard one of the three ships escorted to Virginia by Lord De La Warr, whose July 1610 arrival narrowly averted the abandonment of the colony. Jordan's future wife, Cisley (Sysley, Sisley), arrived in Virginia in 1611 aboard the *Swan*, a vessel in Sir Thomas Gates' fleet, when she was only nine or ten years old. She may have been accompanied by her parents, for Gates' ships brought some 300 men, women, and children to the colony.

Samuel Jordan was living in Virginia when the colony was governed by Sir Thomas Gates and Sir Thomas Dale (1611-1616), who had instituted martial law. In fact, Jordan lived at Bermuda Hundred (Charles City), where Dale himself resided, and probably was there when John Rolfe conducted his famous tobacco experiments and fell in love with Pocahontas. Samuel Jordan and Samuel Sharpe represented Bermuda Hundred's inhabitants in the July-August 1619 meeting of the colony's assembly, the first legislative body of its kind in the New World. Jordan was one of eight men appointed to review the first of four books of laws sent to Virginia, an indication that he was literate.

While relatively little is known about Samuel Jordan's personal background, the Virginia Company compensated him for his service to the colony, which suggests that he was in its employ. It is certain that he was a Company investor. In 1617 Samuel Jordan brought his apprentice, Thomas Matterdy, to Virginia. They had worked together in England, which suggests that one or both men possessed specialized skills. Fragments of crucibles and nonnative minerals unearthed at Jordan's Point, at an archaeological site most likely associated with Samuel Jordan, raise the possibility that he had expertise in chemistry or metallurgy. Jordan may have associated with the Company of Battery Works for Steel and Iron, which Lord De La Warr placed under Captain John Martin's supervision in July 1610. Jordan's arrival date and his lengthy association with Bermuda Hundred, Sir Thomas Dale's home community, raise the possibility that he was among the "hard-liners" who favored a military style of government. Court testimony reveals that Jordan sometimes traded with Dictoris Christmas and with John Pountis, the Virginia Company's vice-admiral who had an interest in the northern fisheries, particularly in the processing of sturgeon. Both men were associated with Smyth's (Southampton) Hundred, a plantation established in 1618-1619 by investors who also were high-ranking Virginia Company officials.

SAMUEL JORDAN'S LANDHOLDINGS

On December 21, 1620, Samuel Jordan received a patent for 450 acres, land to which he was entitled under the headright system. Jordan's first dividend consisted of the 200 acres to which he and his wife, Cisley, were entitled as *ancient planters* plus an additional 250 acres for having transported five people to the colony between 1617 and 1620: John Davis and Thomas Matterdy in 1617, Robert Marshall and Alice Woad in 1619, and Thomas Steed in 1620. Governor Yeardley noted that in recognition for Jordan's service to the colony, his first dividend of land was to be doubled after it had been "seated," that is, developed or placed under cultivation. Thus, Jordan was eligible for an additional 450 acres of land as soon as he had made use of his first claim.

Samuel Jordan's December 1620 patent reveals that his original 450 acres was comprised of three parcels, two of which were in Bermuda Hundred and contained buildings. Jordan's third parcel, a 388-acre tract that had not been seated, was on the north side of the James River, in or near "Sandis his hundred," perhaps a reference to Smyth's Hundred, in which Sir Edwin Sandys had an invested interest. Jordan's 388 acres bordered east upon the land of Temperance Baley and west on that of Captain John Woodlief, whose patents were in the territory known as the Great Weyanoke. Woodlief, who in 1619 had owned land adjacent to Samuel Jordan's at Bermuda Hundred, by December 1620 had relinquished his land on the upper side of the James and patented acreage immediately to the west of Jordan's Point and contiguous to Jordan's patent.

Samuel Jordan, like Woodlief, may have exchanged his right to acreage on the north side of the James River for the parcel at Jordan's Point because much, perhaps all, of the northerly territory was encompassed by four privately-owned plantations (West and Shirley Hundred, Smyth's Hundred, Westover, and Berkeley Hundred) and the Virginia Company's tract of Company Land in Charles City. In fact, in late 1618 Virginia Company officials had ordered incoming Governor George Yeardley make sure that the Berkeley Hundred settlers' 8,000 acre patent did not impinge upon the land that already had been assigned to Smyth's Hundred's investors—100,000 acres that extended from the mouth of the Chickahominy River to Westover.

On the other hand, Samuel Jordan's parcel at Jordan's Point may have been his second dividend of land, acreage he stood to receive once he had seated his first patent. The promontory on which he seated, once home to a sprawling Indian settlement, would have been less troublesome to clear and place under cultivation. In July 1622 Jordan received from Mary Tue a share of Virginia Company stock that entitled him to 100 acres in Digges Hundred, a tract that lay on the north side of the James, just west of the Appomattox

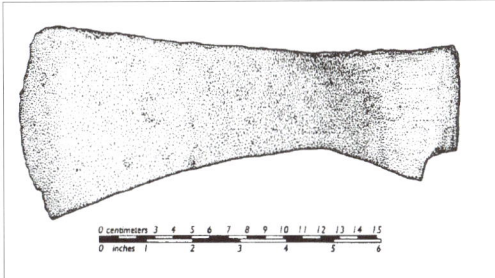

Felling ax from 44PG 300. Drawing by Jamie May.

River's mouth. In May 1625, when a list of the patented land in the colony was sent back to England, Samuel Jordan, who by then was deceased, was credited with 450 acres in the corporation of Charles City, his plantation at Jordan's Point.

THE INDIAN ATTACK

On March 22, 1622, when the Indians of the Powhatan Chiefdom mounted a well planned attack upon the settlements thinly scattered along the banks of the James River, numerous lives were lost, especially in the upper reaches of the James River. At Bermuda or Charles City (today's City Point) and a nearby plantation called Captain Smith's (perhaps the Company Land in Charles City, on which Captain Roger Smith had seated a group of Company servants) thirteen people lay dead. At William Farrar's plantation on the east side of the

The James River in the vicinity of Jordan's Point. Courtesy of Google Earth.

Appomattox River, somewhat inland from Bermuda City, ten people were slain. Some (perhaps all) were Farrar's servants and tenants. At least one man, a husbandman, was from Yorkshire, England.

No one apparently was killed at Samuel Jordan's plantation, Jordan's Journey, or Beggars Bush as it was sometimes called. Likewise, no lives were lost at Captain Isaac Chaplin's plantation, Chaplins Choice, located just east of Jordan's Point, between Jenny and Chappell Creeks. But immediately to Chaplin's east, at William Bikars' house, which was situated upon a point of land on the east side of Chappell Creek, five people were killed, including Bikars himself. To Bikars' east was Powel-Brooke (later, part of Merchants Hope), the settlement established by Captain Nathaniel Powell, where the death toll was twelve. On the north side of the James River, the Indians attacked Nathaniel Causey's plantation, Causey's Clear, and at Berkeley Hundred, eleven people were killed. At neighboring Westover a dozen settlers lost their lives.

JORDAN'S JOURNEY: A POSITION OF STRENGTH

Virginia's governing officials, faced with the loss of more than a third of the colonists' lives, declared martial law and ordered the occupants of outlying plantations to abandon their homes. And soon as they did, the Indians returned to complete their destruction. Eight settlements were strengthened and held, as were a few plantations on the lower side of the James River, across from Jamestown Island. Each was entrusted to a military commander, whose power was absolute in matters of war.

According to Captain John Smith, *"Master Samuel Jordan gathered together but a few of the straglers [sic] about him at Beggers Bush, where he fortified and lived in despight [sic] of the enemy."* Thus, Jordan's Journey, which was made defensible, became a rallying point for survivors of the Indian attack. Four of the eight major strongholds (Flowerdew Hundred, Shirley Hundred, Southampton Hundred, and Jordan's Journey) were located within the corporation of Charles City, probably because of the number of settlers living there. Survivors in the corporation of Henrico, who were placed under the command of Captain Roger Smith, were transported downriver to Pace's Paines and William Ewin's plantation, across from Jamestown Island, or to Kecoughtan (Elizabeth City), at the mouth of the James River. The Indians continued to harass the settlers at Southampton Hundred, which eventually was abandoned. In April 1622 Sir Francis Wyatt, who replaced Sir George Yeardley as governor, sent word to officials in England that "he thought fitt to hold a few outlying places, including the plantation of Mr. Samuel Jordan's." Wyatt closed by asking for arms and armor to use against the Indians.

Ancient planter Nathaniel Causey, whose plantation, Causey's Care, was attacked during the 1622 assault, moved his household to Jordan's Journey. According to Captain John Smith, Causey, "being cruelly wounded, and with the Salvages about him, with an axe did cleave one of their heads, whereby the rest fled and he escaped." Surviving settlers from nearby Berkeley Hundred, Westover, Chaplins Choice, and the Bikars plantation also may have taken refuge at Jordan's Journey, the nearest stronghold. Flowerdew Hundred probably became the safe haven for those fleeing Weyanoke, for both were owned by Sir George Yeardley. Survivors from Martin's Brandon, then leased to Captain William Eppes, were taken to his plantation on the Eastern Shore. The inhabitants of Bermuda Hundred and Bermuda City probably went to Shirley Hundred, for settlement was concentrated at its western limits, directly across the river. William Farrar, in obedience to the governor's orders, would have abandoned his Appomattox River plantation, then unsafe to occupy. He may have gone to Jordan's Journey, bypassing Shirley Hundred, the nearest stronghold, because he and Samuel Jordan were friends.

Above: Eighteenth Century Westover Plantation VDHR photo. Below: Eighteenth Century Shirley Plantation. Photo by David K. Hazzard.

Samuel Jordan's connection with Virginia Company "hard-liners," at least one of whom was a principal investor in the Society of Berkeley Hundred, and the deaths of the Berkeley Hundred plantation's principal leaders, may have prompted him to bring its surviving settlers to Jordan's Journey while awaiting instructions from England. Nineteenth-century historian Alexander G. Brown claimed that Thomas Kemish (Kemis), who succeeded the late William Tracy and George Thorpe as Berkeley Hundred's leader, brought the settlement's cattle to Jordan's Journey shortly after the Indian attack. He was a gentleman and surveyor, who had agreed to work for four years in exchange for 40 acres of land.

In August 1622 John Smyth of Nibley, one of the Society of Berkeley Hundred's main investors, compiled a list of the Berkeley Hundred settlers he believed had survived the Indian attack. It was highly inaccurate, for historical records reveal that he omitted at least sixteen people's names. Richard Milton, Thomas Palmer, John Gibbs, Margaret Finch, Edith Halliers, William Popleton, and Richard Sheriffe Jr., a cooper, went to Jordan's Journey and stayed on, whereas Sheriffe's father, a carpenter in the employ of Berkeley Hundred, died at Jordan's Journey between April 1623 and February 1624. Alexander Bradway and his wife, Sisley, and William Clement (Clements), a cook and gardener, may have gone to Jordan's Journey as evacuees, but sometime prior to February 1624 they took up residence at Bermuda Hundred, where they remained. Thomas Brooks, who arrived in 1623, a few months after the Indian attack, lived briefly at Jordan's Journey but by early 1625 had relocated to Flowerdew Hundred. However, ancient planters Robert Turner, Henry Williams, and Thomas Chapman, who in February 1624 were at Bermuda Hundred, by early 1625 had moved to Jordan's Journey, as did William Nichols and Thomas Ironmonger, who formerly had been at Shirley Hundred. Ten other people (including two nuclear families), who were living at Jordan's Journey in 1624, were gone by early 1625, perhaps having died.

THE PLIGHT OF REFUGEES

Some of the defensive measures Virginia's governing officials took in the wake of the Indian attack increased the colonists' misery, for when they concentrated the population at several sites, they created new sets of problems.

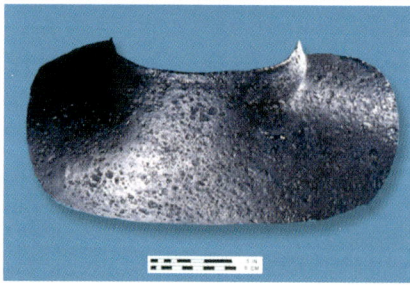

Food shortages were commonplace, a predicament made worse by the arrival of shiploads of new colonists. Sickness also was prevalent, for refugees from some of the settlements at the head of the James River were moved into the territory to the east of the Chickahominy River's mouth. There, the river is especially salty during the summer months, trapping contaminants that spread contagious diseases.

As soon as Virginia Company officials received word of the Indian attacks and learned that many settlements had been abandoned, they demanded that the colonists return to their plantations as soon as possible. Some people undoubtedly were eager to do so, for their economic survival was linked to the land they had developed.

Above: Gorget front plate recovered from 44PG302. VDHR photo. Below: Gorget back plate found in 44PG302. VDHR photo.

In response to the Virginia government's request for arms and ammunition, the Virginia Company obtained weaponry from the Tower of London, an estimated 1,300 firearms. The equipment arrived at Jamestown late in 1622, but the supply was inadequate for Virginia planters living in small and widely scattered communities.

AFTERMATH

By April 1623 Virginia officials sent word to England that "as many returne to theire Plantationes as have desired the same." If refugees from Chaplins Choice and the Bikars plantation took refuge at Jordan's Journey in the wake of the Indian attack, they probably returned home within a year or so. However, the 1624 census and 1625 muster reveal that most of Berkeley Hundred's settlers stayed on at Jordan's Journey, as did Nathaniel Causey and his household. Both groups of refugees were within easy commuting distance of their own property which lay directly across the James River. This would have enabled them to return from time to time to keep their acreage clear of brush and perhaps under cultivation. However, by staying on at Jordan's Journey they would have had the protection that came from living in a defensible community.

Jordan's Point's principal leader, Samuel Jordan, died sometime after April 1623, and on November 19, 1623, his pregnant widow, Cisley, and William Farrar were ordered by the General Court to bring in an account of his estate. By that time, Farrar seems to have made Jordan's Journey his permanent home.

JORDAN'S JOURNEY IN 1624

On February 16, 1624, when a census was taken of the colony's inhabitants, there were forty-two men, women and children living at Jordan's Journey. However, eight settlers had died since April 1623. In 1624 nine nuclear families were living at Jordan's Journey, giving the community an air of permanency. Mrs. Cisley Jordan headed the list, followed by her daughters Mary and Margery or Margaret. William Farrar also was part of Mrs. Jordan's household. To the east, at nearby Chaplins Choice, were twenty-four colonists. Berkeley, Westover, and the Causey and Bikars plantations seem to have been unoccupied.

JORDAN'S JOURNEY IN JANUARY 1625

A muster made on January 21, 1625, reveals that many of the people residing at Jordan's Journey in February 1624 were still there and that a number of new settlers had joined them. The 1625 muster shows the number of households then living at Jordan's Journey, how well they were armed and provisioned, how much livestock they had, and the number of houses and boats that were on hand. The muster-taker usually recorded the names and ages of the men, women and children in each settlement and sometimes made note of when they had come to the colony. Sometimes he set down the names of the vessels on which they had crossed the Atlantic. Servants were identified, household by household, as were "foreigners," that is, individuals who were not English. In January 1625 there were thirty-six males and nineteen females of all ages at Jordan's Journey. Most of the adults were in their twenties and no non-English people were present. On hand were twenty cattle, twenty-four swine, and more than two hundred poultry.

The Jordan's Journey community, which had twenty-two houses, was well prepared to defend itself, for the inhabitants had thirty-four guns and a carbine, ten complete suits of armor, and twenty-six coats of chain mail and headpieces. Archaeological evidence to the contrary, the muster-taker failed to note that fortifications were present, for at least two of Jordan's Point's domestic complexes were protected by palisades. This raises the possibility that the person compiling the records did not consider such protection a real fort. The community was comprised of fifteen households, ten of whom had only one house. The Jordan-Farrar household had five houses, whereas the Palmer, Fisher, Milton, and Causey households had two. The community had two boats and an abundance of stored food, such as barrels of corn and grain, and more than half-a-ton of fish.

Near-neighbor Chaplins Choice was home to seventeen men, women, and children. Five of them had been sent to Virginia by investors in Truelove's Company, whose settlers arrived in 1622, right after the Indian attack. In 1625 the munitions at Chaplins Choice included several "murderers" (small iron or brass ordnance), three of which were "for the forte," and a falconet. However, the muster-taker failed to attribute a fort to Chaplins Choice.

THE RESIDENTS OF JORDAN'S POINT

In January 1625, Mrs. Cisley Jordan (age twenty-four) and William Farrar (age thirty-one) headed the list of households at Jordan's Journey. Their muster included three-year-old Mary Jordan and one-year-old Margaret Jordan, offspring of Cisley's marriage to Samuel Jordan. Also present was seven-year-old Temperance Baley, perhaps Mrs. Jordan's child by a former marriage. Ten servants, all of whom were male and eighty percent of whom were between twenty-one and twenty-six years of age, were members of the Jordan-Farrar household. Most of these men had come to Virginia in 1621 or 1622. Robert Turner, who immigrated in 1619, was living at Bermuda Hundred at the time of the 1624 census, whereas William Hatfield arrived in the colony in 1622 and was at West and Shirley Hundred in 1624. All of the other Jordan-Farrar servants had been at Jordan's Journey in 1624.

In June 1637, when William Farrar's son and heir, William, Jr., asserted a claim to his father's land in Henrico County (a narrow-necked peninsula that eventually became known as Farrar Island), he used as headrights seven of the ten servants attributed to the Jordan-Farrar household in 1625. Thus, these men probably were William Farrar's servants, not those of Cisley Jordan or her late husband, Samuel. Only John Davis, a resident of Jordan's Journey in 1625, can be positively associated with Samuel Jordan, who used him as a headright when obtaining his December 1620 patent. In January 1625 Davis and his partner, William Emmerson, headed a household of their own. John Davis's association with Samuel Jordan raises the possibility that they might have been near-neighbors at Jordan's Point.

Ancient planter Nathaniel Causey went to Virginia in 1607 and came to Jordan's Journey as a refugee in 1622. He and his wife, Thomasine, who had been in the colony since 1609, were living at Jordan's Journey in 1624 and in 1625 were credited with two houses. At least two of the Causeys' five servants came to Virginia at the expense of the Society of Truelove's Company, a group of London-based investors whose settlers arrived in Virginia shortly after the 1622 Indian attack. In January 1625 Nathaniel Causey was given custody of the Truelove Company's material goods, which probably included some of the items the company's investors sent to the colony in August 1621. That shipment included a great iron mortar, a pig of lead, and three iron plates; some butter firkins, saucers, and small forks; six swords and belts; four trunks of apparel; a bundle of kettles; two chests of bottles; and three trunks of bedding. When Nathaniel Causey made a trip to England during the late 1620s, he encountered Captain John Smith who interviewed him about conditions in the colony. Nathaniel and Thomasine Causey stayed on at Jordan's Journey. They retained ownership of their plantation, Causey's Care, which descended to their heir, John Causey, who sold it in 1634.

Thomas Palmer, whose social status was comparable to that of William Farrar, came to Virginia in the *Tiger* in 1621 with his wife, Joan, and daughter, Priscilla. Before the ship left England, Palmer paid Virginia Company officials for some of the goods being sent to Berkeley Hundred, the community with which he was associated, and he was among those who inventoried the estate of George Thorpe, a casualty of the March 1622 Indian attack. In January 1625, when Thomas Palmer was living at Jordan's Point, he had an abundant supply of stored food and defensive weaponry. In his household was eleven-year-old Richard English Jr., a young servant who had arrived in Virginia in the *James* in 1622, immediately after the Indian attack. Richard's father was deceased, as was the male servant who had accompanied them to the colony. By 1629 Thomas Palmer had been placed in command of Shirley Hundred. He represented the community as a burgess and was named a commissioner of the monthly court. Palmer went to England at the end of the year and died there. The bequests he made to his heirs attest to his wealth.

In 1625 Robert Fisher, an ancient planter, shared his Jordan's Point home with his wife, Katherine, and their year-old daughter, Sisley. In 1624 he filed a claim against the estate of George Thorpe, in an attempt to recover payment for the five weeks he had spent building a house for the paramount chief Opechancanough, leader of the 1622 Indian attack. Robert Fisher arrived in Virginia in 1611, when Sir Thomas Gates brought 300 people to the colony. Robert's wife, Katherine, came to the colony in 1621 in the *Marmaduke*, a ship that brought a group of the young, marriageable maids sent to Virginia to become wives for the colonists. She may have been the former Katherine Finch.

John Flood (Fludd), an ancient planter who came to Virginia in 1610, was living at Jordan's Journey in 1625. He was a former servant to Isaac and Jabez Whitaker, who were Virginia Company employees. Flood married Margaret Finch of Berkeley Hundred, whose late husband, William, had been killed there in 1622. The Floods shared their home with her daughter, Frances Finch. By 1630 John Flood had become Flowerdew Hundred's burgess. He was living at Westover in 1639 but eventually moved to Surry County. Flood, who was fluent in the Algonquian language, was involved in Indian trade and was instrumental in negotiating the 1646 treaty.

John Clay, who also was an ancient planter, was living at Jordan's Journey in 1625. He shared a home with his wife, Ann, and a male servant, William Nicholas, a former inmate of England's Bridewell Prison. Clay, a successful planter, patented some land of his own in 1635 and seems to have moved away. Ancient planter Thomas Chapman, who was living at Jordan's Journey in 1624 and 1625, was one of Captain Robert Smalley's former servants in the corporation of Henrico. Chapman's wife, Ann, owned some land on the lower side of the James River, in Elizabeth City. Henery (Henry) Williams, an ancient planter who in 1624 and 1625 was living at Jordan's Journey, by 1635 had moved to the Eastern Shore.

Other households in the Jordan's Journey settlement included those of John Gibbs and his partner Christopher Safford, who in 1624 had been a married man. Gibbs, one of the Society of Berkeley Hundred's men, was a former servant of Arnold Oldisworth and had accompanied him to Virginia. Edith Halliers, William Popleton, Richard Milton, Richard Sheriffe Sr. (a carpenter), and Richard Sheriffe Jr. (a cooper), all of whom were associated with Berkeley Hundred, also went to Jordan's Journey and stayed on. Other residents of Jordan's Point included William and Ann Branlin, plus several small all-male households. Many of the men and women who were indentured servants at Jordan's Journey in 1625 came to the colony in 1622 or 1623.

The presence of young children suggests that by 1624 the community was taking on a semblance of permanency. Edward Clarke, his wife, and their child, had been at Jordan's Journey in 1624 but were not present in 1625. Whether the Clarkes died, relocated, or were simply overlooked remains a mystery. Of the community's six all-male households, only two had servants.

William Besse (Basse), a yeoman farmer who had lived in the Bermuda Islands for six years before coming to Virginia, was a girdler originally from St. Mildred Poultry, in London. He arrived sometime after 1621 and in February 1624 was living at Jordan's Journey. Besse and his wife returned briefly to England, but in 1626 he identified himself as a tobacco planter and resident of Jordan's Journey. He survived until at least 1640, at which time he shipped tobacco from Virginia to Rotterdam.

THE BERKELEY CONNECTION

At least eleven of the people living at Jordan's Journey in 1624 and 1625 came to Virginia at the expense of the Society of Berkeley Hundred, a group of investors from Gloucestershire, England. The Society's members included Richard Berkeley, Sir William Throgmorton, John Smyth of Nibley, and their asso-

Eighteenth Century Berkeley Plantation. VDHR photo.

ciates. Berkeley and Throgmorton, who lived near Bristol, England, were close kinsmen of Sir Thomas Dale's widow, Lady Elizabeth, who owned land on West and Shirley Hundred (Eppes) Island, across the James River from Jordan's Journey.

The Society of Berkeley Hundred outfitted its first group of settlers and sent them to Virginia in the *Margaret*, which left Bristol, England, on September 16, 1619, and arrived at Old Point Comfort on November 30. The newcomers, then under the command of Captain John Woodlief, included gentlemen, husbandmen, and several skilled workers (a gunmaker, a gardener, a smith, a joiner, a tailor, and two carpenters), who were outfitted with the tools of their trade. They were tenants who had agreed to work for the Society of Berkeley Hundred for a certain number of years in exchange for an agreed-upon quantity of land. At least two people in the first group of Berkeley Hundred settlers were Virginia Company servants, whose passage had been paid by the Society of Berkeley Hundred.

Two coopers were sent to Berkeley Hundred and survived the 1622 Indian attack. Courtesy of the National Park Service, Colonial National Historical Park, Jamestown Collection.

Shortly after the Berkeley Hundred colonists arrived in Virginia, they went to the land the Society had been assigned, on the north side of the James River, between the plantations called Westover and West and Shirley Hundred. Captain John Woodlief, then Berkeley Hundred's commander, was told to see that "home-like" houses were built for the settlers, along with two sturdily framed buildings: one for worship and the other for the storage of weapons, tools, and provisions. Woodlief also was ordered to see that 400 acres of grazing land were enclosed with a strong palisade.

Early in 1620 there was a change in the Berkeley Hundred plantation's leadership, for William Tracy acquired Sir William Throgmorton's financial interest in the property. In March 1620, several men set sail in the *London Merchant*. They were followed in September by William Tracy and several other gentlemen, some with their wives and children, who left Bristol in the *Supply*. Also aboard were a clergyman, two experienced ironworkers, and some of the supplies the settlers needed when becoming established.

In August 1621 a fourth group of Berkeley Hundred settlers set out in the *Tiger*, the *Marmaduke*, and the *Warwick*. Thomas Palmer, who was aboard the *Tiger*, paid Virginia Company officials for nails, food stuffs (such as oatmeal, oil, and peas), iron pots for cooking, and utilitarian vessels, such as pudding

pans, porridge dishes, pipkins, baking pans, and chamber pots. A container of boots and shoes, fowling pieces, several trunks, and clothing were aboard the ships, along with passengers. One man whose clothing needs were supplied by the Society of Berkeley Hundred was furnished with a doublet and hose, a cloth suit, two pair of stockings, a canvas suit that was lined, a rug, and a pair of knit stockings. Another man, who was a community leader, was outfitted more amply. Besides clothing, he was provided with fish hooks, two swords, some small porcelain dishes, a copper still, a brass baking pan, and a case of bottles. Despite an alarming death toll, the Berkeley Hundred settlement was well established by the time of the March 1622 Indian attack, at which time eleven people were killed. Afterward, the survivors

Early seventeenth century sgraffito jug from Donyatt, South Somerset, U.K. Photo by Taft Kaiser.

probably took refuge at Samuel Jordan's plantation, known as a position of strength. The 1624 census and 1625 muster reveal that at least eleven of the people then living at Jordan's Journey were former residents of Berkeley Hundred.

In June 1624 Richard Milton and John Gibbs testified in court about debts against the estate of Captain George Thorpe of Berkeley, who had been killed in the Indian attack. In January 1625 Milton, who had come to Virginia in 1620 in the *Supply* and had accompanied settlement leader William Tracy, was ordered to move to Shirley Hundred to tend to Berkeley Hundred's cattle. Robert Fisher, mean-

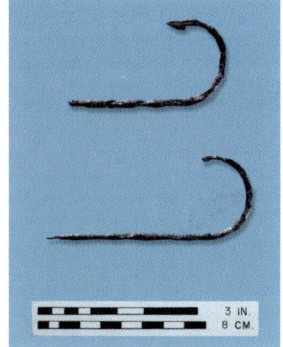

Fishhooks were among the utilitarian items sent to Berkeley Hundred. VDHR photo.

while, was paid from the late George Thorpe's estate for building a house for Opechancanough. In 1627 William Farrar was ordered to make an accounting of Berkeley Hundred's cattle and several years later, when he was in England, he conferred with the Society of Berkeley Hundred's investors about the future of their settlement. He would have had reliable information, obtained from the Berkeley Hundred settlers then living at Jordan's Journey.

In essence, the March 22, 1622, Indian attack signaled the Berkeley Hundred community's demise. On August 1, 1622, John Smyth of Nibley, one of the Society of Berkeley Hundred's principal investors, reported that only thirteen or four-teen of their settlers were still alive. They would have included Thomas, Joan, and Pricilla Palmer, John Gibbs, Richard Milton, Margaret Finch Flood and her daughter, Frances Finch, William Popleton, Edith Halliers, Richard Sheriffe Sr. and his son, Richard Jr., Alexander Bradway and his wife, Sisley, and William Clement. The names of a few other people known to have survived the Indian attack were omitted from the 1624 census and the 1625 muster. They were John Blanchard, a gentleman; Thomas Molton, a cook and gardener; George Hale, a drummer; Thomas Kemis, a surveyor and gentleman; and Christopher

Small handmade lead dice found at 44PG300, perhaps made from discarded lead shot. VDHR photo.

Bourton, a tailor. Some or all of these individuals probably moved to Jordan's Journey after the Indian attack and died there before demographic records were compiled in February 1624. John Smyth of Nibley noted that three new people had set sail for Virginia in June 1622 and a fourth was departing in August, but he failed to mention their names. In light of their time of arrival, they may have gone directly to Jordan's Journey.

In July 1623 when some Virginia Company investors resolved to send supplies to the colony, for the relief of surviving settlers, John Smyth of Nibley indicated that he was dispatching aid to his "servants now living in Virginia in Berkeley Hundred and such others as this next August I send over to increase them." Thus, Smyth seems to have been unaware that the surviving Berkeley Hundred settlers had abandoned their sponsors' property. After Smyth learned that the Berkeley Hundred acreage had been vacated, he did not send additional people to Virginia, although in April 1623 he did ship over a modest quantity of wheat meal, peas, and oatmeal. On May 24, 1624, when the Virginia Company's charter was revoked, many of those who had invested in the colonization of Virginia were left to ponder what the future might hold. It is probable that the Society of Bermuda Hundred's investors were among them.

HE SAID, SHE SAID

The minutes of the colony's General Court for 1624 and 1625 provide us with a fleeting glimpse of everyday life at Jordan's Journey, for Cisley, the wealthy widow of settlement leader Samuel Jordan, became embroiled in a breach of promise suit filed by a spurned suitor. Several neighbors provided testimony. Their sworn statements reveal much about the texture life on the Virginia frontier.

According to court testimony, only three or four days after Cisley Jordan was widowed, the Rev. Grivell Pooly (Pooley), the minister who served Flowerdew Hundred, Jordan's Journey, Chaplins Choice, and Shirley Hundred, expressed

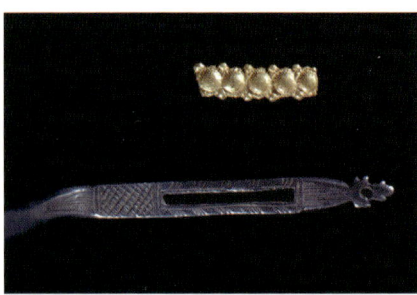

an interest in marrying her. When Captain Isaac Madison of West and Shirley Hundred Island approached Cisley on Pooly's behalf, inquiring whether she would consider the match, she said that "she would not marry any man until she was delivered," an indication that she was pregnant at the time of her late husband's death. Pooly quickly set his plans in motion and in front of Captain Madison and his wife, Mary,

A fragment of a gold finger ring (top) and the decorated end of a silver bodkin, both from the seventeenth century, recovered at archaeological site 44PG302, Jordan's Point.

he and Cisley Jordan purportedly pledged to wed, kissed, and drank a toast to seal their bargain. According to Pooly, Mrs. Jordan insisted that their engagement be kept secret, because her late husband's death was so recent. She, on the other hand, later declared that she intended to marry William Farrar and denied that she ever had been engaged to Grivell Pooly. Mary Madison and her servant, John Harris, testified in court that Mrs. Jordan had confided that Pooly would have fared far better had he not revealed their plans.

If a rumor spread by community gossip Joan Vinsone was true, Cisley's marriage to Samuel Jordan was an unhappy one on account of his love for Alice

Boyse, a married woman and resident of Bermuda Hundred. Ultimately, the governor and council concluded that they were unable to render a decision in the breach of promise case and forwarded the matter to officials in England.

In January 1625, when the governor's council, sitting as a court, reopened the case of Pooly vs. Jordan, Nathaniel Causey of Jordan's Journey testified that Mrs. Palmer (another resident of the community) had told him about Mrs. Cisley Jordan's having a vision in which she saw ghostly hands upon her head and that of her child and heard a voice cry out *"Judgment, judgment."* Causey admitted that although he had not been privy to Mrs. Jordan's spiritual experience, he *had* seen Mrs. Jordan and William Farrar kiss and believed it inappropriate for an unmarried couple to be living together. Although the General Court again deferred action, pending advice from England, ultimately the Rev. Grivell Pooly withdrew his bill of complaint and signed a release, absolving Mrs. Jordan of all former contracts and obligations. By May 1625 Cisley Jordan and William Farrar had wed.

WILLIAM FARRAR'S GROWING PRESTIGE

William Farrar played a relatively important role in the political life of the colony. A stockholder in the Virginia Company, he was cousin to Nicholas Farrar, a leading member of that group and a prosperous merchant. In March 1626 William Farrar was appointed to the Council of State, upon which he served for the remainder of his life. In August 1626 he was named a commissioner "for the Upper Parts kept above Persie's Hundred," with the authority to decide whether court would be held at Jordan's Journey or Shirley Hundred.

Farrar apparently chose to have the local court convene at his own home in Jordan's Journey, for it was in session there when two men allegedly uttered the inflammatory words that led to their being brought before the General Court at Jamestown in September 1626. According to eyewitnesses, when a proclamation was read at the monthly court at William Farrar's house, to the effect that only merchants were authorized to go aboard

Case bottle found at 44PG302. VDHR photo.

ships to buy commodities, Richard Taylor and Sergeant Samuel Sharpe made what were considered treasonous statements. Nathaniel Causey, Elmer Phillips and John Crowdick testified that the accused men had, indeed, created a disturbance, but that Taylor and Sharpe were drunk when the incident occurred. That drinking was in progress while court was in session provides insight into the tenor of early seventeenth-century life. Perhaps significantly, an abundance of upscale drinking vessel fragments were found at 44PG302, the archaeological site identified as William Farrar's domestic complex.

In October 1626, when the colony's General Court convened at Jamestown, one of Samuel Sharpe's indentured servants, Henry Carman, who had committed

Yellow silk galloon from 44PG302. VDHR photo.

a sexual offense at Flowerdew Hundred, was ordered to serve seven additional years. Carman, a former inmate of Bridewell Prison, was put into William Farrar's custody while Sharpe was out of the country, although his earnings went to his master. In January 1627, Farrar, as a member of the Council of State, was assigned custody of Thomas North and John Heiny, former tenants of the defunct Virginia Company. In March 1629, William Farrar again was appointed to the court serving the upper James River settlements. Two of his fellow justices were Thomas Palmer and Captain John Davis, former neighbors at Jordan's Journey.

OTHER JORDAN'S JOURNEY RESIDENTS DURING THE 1620s

William Emmerson and John Davis, who in January 1625 jointly headed a Jordan's Journey household, appeared before the colony's General Court in December 1624 and said that they had purchased a servant named William Popleton from Lieutenant John Gibbs. Davis, though listed among the men Samuel Jordan had transported to the colony, was an adventurer in the Virginia Company and was from St. Giles Cripplegate, in London. In 1629 he represented Jordan's Journey in the colony's assembly.

Edward Temple, who was living at West and Shirley Hundred Island in 1624 and 1625, was then described as a servant of Richard Biggs. By January 1627 Temple was working for a Mr. Douglas, a mariner, who gave him written permission to leave Jordan's Journey and to plant at Martin's Brandon. He probably was an indentured servant whose owner leased him to other planters.

A number of the men who were at Jordan's Journey in 1625 went on to attain prominence and establish plantations of their own. William Popleton, who was John Davis's servant in 1625, was serving as a burgess for Jordan's Journey in 1629. The following year, Walter Price represented Jordan's Journey and Chaplins Choice, the community in which he had lived since 1625. John Freme and John Clay patented land to the east of Jordan's Journey, near Wards Creek, and William Dawson, who in 1625 was a servant in the household headed by

William Farrar and Cisley Jordan, by 1635 had purchased 150 acres in what became Isle of Wight County. Indian trader John Flood in 1630 served as Flowerdew Hundred's burgess and in 1638 patented 2,100 acres in what became Surry County.

Most of these individuals transported others to the colony, thereby enhancing the amount of acreage to which they were entitled. In July 1627 the settlers of Jordan's Journey, Shirley Hundred, Chaplins Choice, and Peirseys (Flowerdew) Hundred banded together to mount an expedition against the Weyanoke and Appomattock Indian towns, a march that was to commence on August 1. Thus, all of those communities were still viable.

In 1629 Captain John Smith reported that he had interviewed three Virginia planters who were visiting England, about current conditions in the colony. Nathaniel Causey, John Davis, William Emerson, and John Flood, all of whom had been living at Jordan's Journey in January 1625, said that there were around 5,000 Virginia colonists and that livestock and provisions were available in abundance.

THE END OF AN ERA

In April 1631, William Farrar went to England to assist in settling his father's estate. At issue was some real estate in which William and his brother, Harry, had inherited a joint interest. Prior to that time, William Farrar and his wife, Cisley, had had two children, Cisley and William, whose names were mentioned in their late grandfather's will. Around 1632 the Farrars' son, John, was born.

While William Farrar was in England, he paid a visit to Thomas Combe, to whom he delivered a written account of Berkeley Hundred's cattle. The list, compiled by Richard Milton, who had been responsible for the herd for the last few years, stated that there were twenty-three cattle that were owned by John Smith of Nibley and Richard Berkeley.

An unsigned note, probably written by John Smyth of Nibley, was appended to the document William Farrar presented to Thomas Combe. It stated that shortly before Farrar set sail for England, Virginia Governor John Harvey had commenced confiscating cattle whose owners did not live in Virginia, claiming that he was acting on the king's behalf. The anonymous writer indicated that Harvey had promised some of the Society of Berkeley Hundred's cattle to Captain Francis Eppes and the Rev. Roland Graine, a clergyman. He also said that Thomas Palmer, who had accompanied William Farrar to England, admitted having one of Berkeley Hundred's heifers in his possession. The writer added that for many years, Richard Milton had kept Berkeley Hundred's cattle at West and Shirley Hundred Island, whose owners had complained to Governor Harvey about the animals' presence.

The writer went on to describe Berkeley Hundred's location and its boundaries. He said that when William Farrar returned to Virginia, he was to be accompanied by John Gibbs who carried letters to Virginia's governor and council. He added that if Gibbs and Richard Milton would agree to reoccupy the Society of Berkeley Hundred's property, more settlers would be sent over and placed under their supervision and they would be given the Society's cattle.

In June 1632 Thomas Combe, who went to Virginia briefly and then returned to England, dispatched a letter to John Smyth of Nibley. He stated that Richard Milton preferred not to have a partner but was willing to oversee three of the Society's servants, if he were sent three of his own. Combe said that he considered John Gibbs more capable than Richard Milton, but that Gibbs had agreed to work for William Farrar for a year and therefore was not available. Combe added that Gibbs wanted to purchase some of the Society of Berkeley Hundred's land and cattle and become a planter in his own right. Thomas Combe sought other Society members' opinions as to how Milton and Gibbs should be dealt with, but said that he thought it advantageous to proceed now rather than later.

By August 1633 Richard Berkeley, John Smyth of Nibley, and several others had agreed to commit some funds to reviving Berkeley Hundred. However the sums pledged were very modest and the project never got underway. Thus, the Berkeley Hundred settlers who moved to Jordan's Journey in the wake of the 1622 Indian attack never returned to their plantation.

On February 9, 1637, Governor John Harvey issued a patent to a syndicate of London merchants and mariners, assigning them 8,000 acres called Berkeley Hundred. The patent stated that "the Adventurers and Company of Berkeley Hundred" had conveyed the land to the new owners, all of whom had long-term involvement in Virginia commerce. Later, the merchants who bought Berkeley Hundred purchased Martin's Brandon.

William Farrar died sometime prior to June 11, 1637, at which time his son and namesake repatented his land in Henrico County, the tract that became known as Farrar Island. During the 1630s, when colonists patented land both east and west of Jordan's Point, the headlands at the point were still identified as Beggars Bush or Jordan's, even though Samuel Jordan had been dead for more than a decade. If the Jordans' daughters, Mary and Margaret, lived to maturity, they would have inherited the tract. If not, it would have escheated to the Crown. The lengthy and uninterrupted association of the Jordan's Point patent with Samuel Jordan implies that it remained in his family, but the name may merely have been a deeply ingrained tradition.

THE JORDAN'S POINT NEIGHBORHOOD

In 1635 Thomas Causey claimed 150 acres in the Indian field, "commonly so called," that abutted north upon Jordans Journey, west on the main woods, south on Chaplins Choice and east upon the main river. Causey's patent suggests that Jenny or Bickers Creek formed the southeasterly bounds of Jordans Journey. In 1637, John Woodlief or Woodlife, whose land bordered north upon the James

River, received the title to 530 acres "near the headland called Beggars Bush." His acreage abutted east upon Samuel Jordan's plantation and extended southward into the mainland; a year later he received an additional 200 acres that lay inland and contiguous to his 530 acres and abutted west upon the patent of Francis Poythress. Woodlief's 1637 patent reaffirmed his right to some property he had acquired earlier on, twenty acres in Charles or Bermuda Hundred, a parcel that abutted south upon land that had been assigned to Samuel Jordan in December 1620. Likewise, a 1645 patent for some land in Henrico County makes reference to some land that was attributed to John Woodlief and Samuel Jordan on the north side of the James River. In 1638, Edward Hill of Shirley Hundred patented 450 acres behind Samuel Jordan's land at Jordan's Point. Hill's acreage abutted north upon Jordan's headlands, east upon Chaplins Choice, west upon John Woodlief's patent, and south into the main.

Seventeenth century gloves embellished with silver metal-wrapped thread and spangles. Courtesy of the Agecroft Association. Photo by Jefferson Collins.

CHAPTER 5

The Archaeology of Jordan's Journey

INTRODUCTION

During archaeological excavations at Jordan's Point, the remains of Jordan's Journey, a substantial early seventeenth century settlement, were unearthed. The community included the sites designated 44PG300, 44PG302, 44PG307, and a portion of 44PG151. At least two households at Jordan's Journey occupied domestic complexes that were fortified. Other subsurface cultural features associated with early seventeenth century occupation at Jordan's Point await discovery unless they have been destroyed by modern development.

Although it is tempting to assume that when demographic records were collected during the 1620s, the compiler went from house to house, like a modern census taker, such was not the case. Historical research on landowner-ship patterns in urban Jamestown, where small lots were aligned in rows along two streets paralleling the waterfront, demonstrates clearly that in early 1625 when a muster was compiled of the colony's inhabitants, political and social rank reigned supreme. Thus, the household of the governor (the highest ranking official) was listed first, followed by that of the former governor, and other men of distinction, whose names were set down in descending order. Only those of lesser—but comparable— standing were listed without heed to status. When demographic records were compiled at other substantial settlements, such as Flowerdew Hundred, Hog Island, Westover, the Governor's Land, and Martin's Hundred, the household attributable to settlement's principal leader was listed first, followed by those of other prominent citizens and people of lesser rank. Thus, the order in which households are listed in the census and muster reflect rank and status, not physical placement within the cultural landscape. For this reason, other criteria must be used when attributing archaeological sites to specific households.

44PG302

A Fortified Compound or Bawn

Between 1990 and 1993 archaeologists from VCU undertook excavations at 44PG302, a large site on the west side of Jordan's Point that covers approximately an acre-and-a-half of land. They discovered eleven early colonial structures that were situated within a long-and-narrow fortified compound or bawn that measured approximately 260 feet in length (north to south) and 110 feet in width (east to west) and was roughly pentagonal. The walls of the palisade were fabricated of posts, pales, and rails, with most of the posts spaced at twelve and a half foot intervals. The exception was the palisade's northern wall, where posts were set only nine feet apart. This suggests that the wall may have been somewhat higher than the others. The northernmost tip or apex of the fortifications at 44PG302, located at the highest point on the landform, seems to have served as a bastion that had a firing step or observation platform. There may have been a gate in the northwestern side of the apex and another gate at the opposing corner of the fort.

Five of the buildings enclosed within the large palisade at 44PG302 were elongated rectangular structures and resembled the types of houses often found within English forts. Such "longhouses" usually were three or more times as long as they were wide and usually were only one room deep. The archaeological evidence at 44PG302 fails to reveal whether these buildings were a story or two in height, or perhaps had a loft above the first floor. Two of the six smaller structures at 44PG302 probably were servant or tenant houses, whereas the remainder may have been used for storage. All eleven buildings at 44PG302 were of frame construction, earthfast structures that were erected upon posts set into the ground. Most of the cultural features at 44PG302 contained large quantities of daub. Thus, these timber houses probably were constructed with walls and hooded hearths or chimneys that were built of lath (or wattles) that had been daubed with clay or clay and lime. Shallow trenches into which the builders of 44PG302 laid wooden sills at ground level, were interrupted by the posts needed to lend support to walls. By burying the structures' walls slightly beneath the surface of the ground, the builders would have been able to keep wind, water, dust, and vermin out of their houses.

Large quantities of nails were found at 44PG302, along with substantial numbers of woodworking tools. Archaeologists are certain that the houses were roofed with wood. They also believe that most exterior surfaces were clad with sawn or riven boards and that some buildings had wood-paneled interiors. Because most of the buildings at Jordan's Point were erected by ancient planters, who were keenly aware of the Virginia climate's effects upon clay walls and wood thatching, they probably opted for an architectural form they knew was sturdier and more durable, especially when a good supply of nails was available.

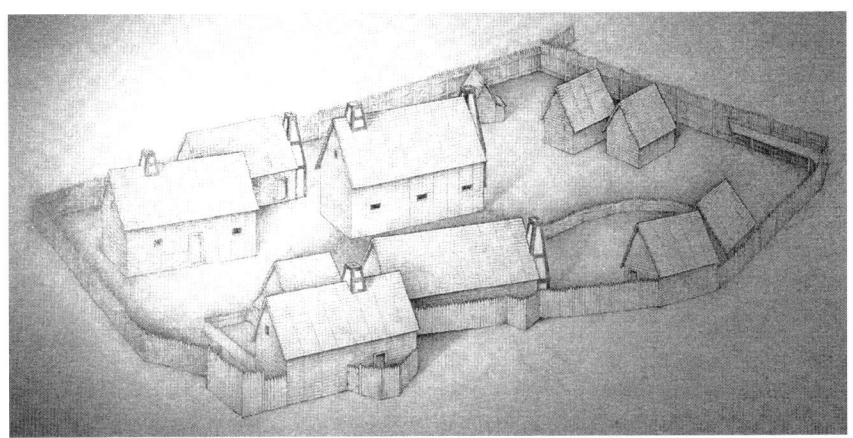

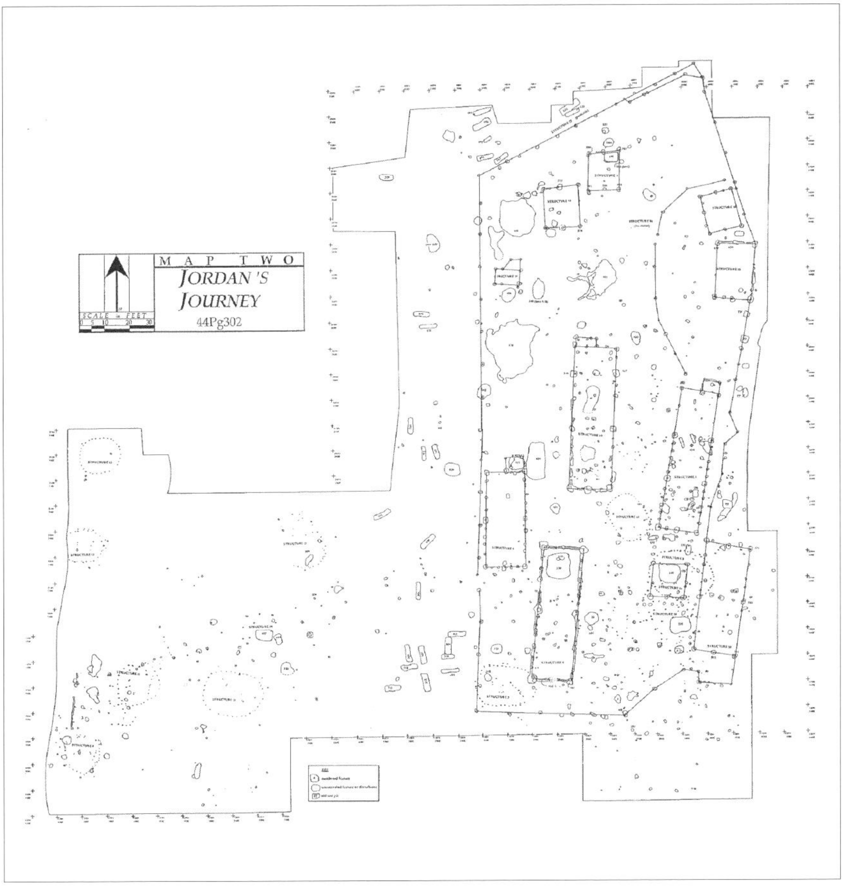

Top: VCU archaeologists' interpretation of 44PG302 based on cultural features mapped at the site (bottom).

Archaeological and historical evidence converge to suggest that 44PG302 is associated with the household of Jordan's Journey settlement leader William Farrar, who in January 1625 was credited with five houses, ten male servants, and a herd of livestock. Significantly, 44PG302's location on the west side of Jordan's Point, would have provided Farrar and his predecessor, Samuel Jordan, with a clear view up the James River, the direction from which attacking Indians might be expected to come.

Ivor Noel Hume, on the basis of his archaeological research at Martin's Hundred, astutely observed that there were similarities between the spatial organization of Virginia's "particular" or private plantations and the early plantations of Northern Ireland. More recently archaeologist Charles Hodges found that pattern replicated at Flowerdew Hundred. Pursuing this analogy, VCU archaeologists surmised that the settlement at Jordan's Point, which in early 1625 was headed by William Farrar, resembled the village called Vintners at Balleague in Ulster, Northern Ireland. The settlement at Vintners was rimmed with defensive works and the manor house of its principal leader was at the heart of community life. His home, which was fortified, included public and private space in which church services were held, court convened, and public business was conducted. A lane that extended through the fortified compound defined the town commons, whereas a road led from the gate to a landing on the river. Individual house lots that included tenants' outbuildings, garden plots, and yards lined the main lane. Some of these dwellings were enclosed by defensive palisades.

Historical records reveal that at Jordan's Point, there were fourteen households of tenants and their servants whose homes were subsidiary to the fortified manor house of the settlement's principal leader. The same type of organizational plan seems to have been in use at nearby Flowerdew Hundred, where Sir George Yeardley's men built a 235 foot long palisade much like the one at Jordan's Point.

Structure 1, the largest house within the fortified compound, likely was the home of Jordan's Journey's founder, Samuel Jordan, and his successor, William Farrar. It was a three-bay longhouse that was fifty-five feet long and sixteen feet wide and was oriented on a north-south axis. All three bays, which were evenly spaced, probably had wooden floors. The middle bay seems to have had a hearth and hooded chimney. At the northern end of the house was a shed that was five or six feet wide and had an internal partition. Food, such as flour, grain, and other perishables, may have been stored there to keep them safe from vermin and moisture. Just outside the house and close to the eastern palisade wall were two small posts that probably supported a step, perhaps an observation post or firing position.

The main dwelling at 44PG302 was closely associated with two other buildings. One was a stable or sturdily built cow barn. The other, a strongly fabricated square structure, is believed to have been an agricultural service building. Because very few nails were found in association with it, archaeologists concluded that the building had wattle and daub walls and a low, shed-like thatched roof. Agricultural tools and items associated with animal husbandry may have been stored there.

Structure 20, a longhouse whose back wall was incorporated into the compound's palisade, may have served as quarters for the Jordan and Farrar household's servants or as a building in which tobacco was cured that perhaps saw use as a gatehouse or trading post. Structure 21, a small, square outbuilding containing a root cellar, was connected with the southern end of Structure 1 by a fenced yard and work area that may have served as a livestock enclosure. Structure 4, a longhouse measuring fifty-one feet by sixteen feet, was divided into three rooms of unequal size. The middle room (or hall) was heated, as was an adjoining room that contained a cellar or buttery. Structure 4 probably had a second story and loft and may have been built early in the site's occupancy by European colonists.

Also present at 44PG302 was Structure 5, a house that measured thirty-six feet by sixteen feet and abutted the fortified compound's western curtain wall. Large but shallowly set posts on the east side of the building defined two entrances that were symmetrically placed. One provided access to a large hall or gathering space that was heated by a fireplace situated in its southernmost wall. The other entryway led into a "parlor," a room that had a large hearth and exterior chimney attached to its north wall. Food probably was prepared in this "parlor" and other utilitarian activities may have occurred there. At the end of the building was a large shed that may have been divided into two rooms.

Structure 15, located at a turn in the palisade wall, was exceptionally sturdy and was located within a livestock enclosure. Therefore it probably served as a shed or stable, although it could have been used as a tobacco barn. VCU archaeologists concluded that Structure 17, a small earthfast building with a cellar, may have been a house that predated the palisade erected at 44PG302. Numerous domestic artifacts were recovered from Structure 17's cellar, where pieces of military equipment and Native American ceramics also were found.

Cultural Materials

A substantial quantity of decorative beads of various colors and shapes were found at 44PG302, along with buttons of brass and black glass and brass and iron hooks and eyes. Archaeologists recovered the metal points or aiglets that would have been at the end of laces or ribbons used to fasten clothing. Cord containing gold and silver threads also was retrieved from the site. All of these items reflect the wealth of those who lived at 44PG302, most likely the home of Samuel and Cisley Jordan and William Farrar, Samuel's successor as husband and community commander. A silver bodkin (a decorative hair pin used to fasten a cap to a woman's head), part of an elaborately decorated gold finger ring, and some gold braid that probably adorned a woman's gloves were found at the site. They most likely belonged to Cisley Jordan Farrar, who in early 1625 was the only adult female in her household.

A tiny black glass sphere, decorated with small, white prunts or rounds of glass, was excavated at 44PG302 and according to curator Beverley Straube, may have been part of an earring. A plain brass band finger ring with traces of gilding also was recovered. Cord, wrapped with threads of silver and gold, was found at the site as were pieces of embroidery interwoven with silver strands and spangles. A fiber band woven from yellow silk and finished with threads wrapped with silver foil, also was unearthed and has been identified as a piece of galloon or decorative trim. According to a 1621 law, only members of the governor's council and the heads of settlements were allowed to wear clothing decorated with gold. Therefore, some of these items probably adorned the personal apparel of Samuel Jordan, William Farrar, or wife Cisley.

Fragments of costly ceramics and elegant glassware reflect the wealth and superior social status of the Jordan-Farrar household. Pieces of numerous porcelain vessels were unearthed at 44PG302, mostly cups that would have been used for drinking beverages. Five of the nine small cups that were found were matching and probably were part of a set. All of these delicate drinking vessels would have been used for sipping wine or tea. A sherd of a large porcelain storage jar was discovered, perhaps a container in which the settlement leader may have stored his personal supply of tobacco. Fragments of similar vessels were found at Flowerdew Hundred at a site archaeologists believe was associated with wealthy merchant and community leader Abraham Peirsey.

Site 44PG302 probably was at the hub of the Jordan's Journey community's social activity. William Farrar, the settlement's commander for more than a decade, would have hosted gatherings of high-ranking officials and local court justices would have convened in his home. Westerwald jugs or pitchers may have been used to convey wine or other alcoholic beverages from cask to cup. A tiny Westerwald jug found at site, the size of a personal drinking vessel, would have been a very costly and high status piece of tableware.

Among the other finds at 44PG302 were lead-glazed redwares, Iberian storage jars and costrels (jugs with handles), Westerwald jugs, Bartman bottles, and tin-enameled wares, vessels that originated in England, the Netherlands, Germany, Italy, Spain, France, and China. But Virginia-made vessels also were found. Nearly a fourth of the ceramic vessels recovered from the site were associated with food and beverage consumption, whereas nearly forty percent would have been used for food preparation and storage. A large number of the vessels unearthed (around eleven percent) would have been associated with medicinal use.

a.

b.

c.

d.

Artifacts found at 44PG302: a. Yellow silk embroidery, VDHR photo.; b. Silver bodkin, Drawing by Jamie May; c. Necks of Westerwald jugs, VDHR photo.; d. Bone knife handle, VDHR photo.

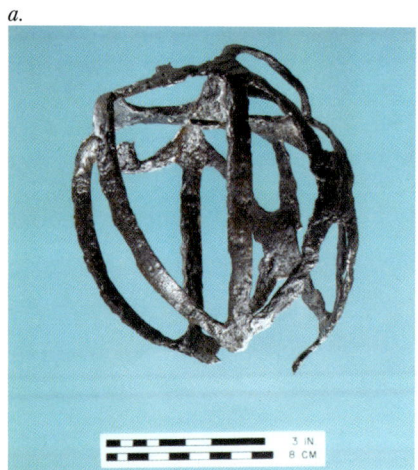

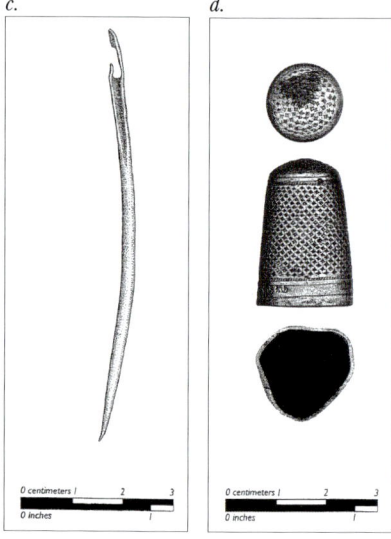

Artifacts found at 44PG302: a. Remains of a sword basket hilt, VDHR photo; b. Seal-top spoon, VDHR photo; c. Cast round-sectioned needle, Drawing by Jamie May; d. Brass thimble, Drawing by Jamie May; e. Brass skimmer, VDHR photo.

Some of the artifacts found at 44PG302 reflect the dangers of frontier living in early seventeenth-century Virginia. The presence of pommels and blades of swords, daggers, and sabers, along with locks and hardware for muskets with snaphaunce and matchlock firing mechanisms, musket barrels, shot, and sprue (waste metal from casting lead shot), attest to the settlers' need to protect themselves and their community. Hundreds of fragments of protective attire, such as chain mail and plate armor, were found as were portions of helmets and tassets (plate armor to protect the upper thigh) and parts of a brigandine, a breastplate, and a gorget.

Culinary utensils were found at 44PG302 as were tools for farming and carpentry. At least four or five saws (including one that probably was of Dutch origin) were unearthed, as was a large two-man (crosscut) saw. Among the large number of hand tools were chisels, a draw knife, hoes, axes, and a carpenter's compass, along with a wide assortment of brass, iron, and pewter objects. A surprisingly large number of bricks were unearthed at the site, along with a lime kiln. These features suggest that some of the settlers at 44PG302 planned to undertake some masonry construction.

Thimbles, brass alloy and iron needles, and a pair of scissors were found at 44PG302, as were nearly 350 straight pins. Several leaden cloth seals, the type usually affixed to bolts of cloth to attest to its quality, quantity, and place of origin, were recovered from 44PG302.

Tip of a seal-top spoon inscribed with an "X," often signifying "Chi" or "Christopher." Drawing by Jamie May, VDHR photo.

Two of those seals indicate that the cloth to which they were attached was defective, raising the possibility that the colonists were sent goods of inferior quality. While some of the cloth may have been considered trade goods, most of it probably was used to fabricate clothing for those who lived at Jordan's Journey. Christopher Bourton, a tailor who survived the Indian attack upon Berkeley Hundred, like others in the community, probably moved to Jordan's Journey. Perhaps significantly, the terminal end of spoons found at 44PG302 and 44PG300 are incised with an "X," a symbol used to signify "Chi" or the first part of the name "Christopher," typically abbreviated as "Xopher" in written records.

The discovery of a flute or whistle that had been fabricated from bone indicates that someone at 44PG302 enjoyed music as a diversion. Some of the colonists who lived at the site were literate and archaeologists recovered brass book hasps, metal fasteners that would have held together the pages of a book. A bone comb also was unearthed.

Two fragments of a stoneware crucible also were found and may have been associated with metallurgical activities undertaken by Samuel Jordan or William Farrar on behalf of the Virginia Company of London, for the early colonists were supposed to search for precious metals. Piedmont schists and gneisses from the western piedmont, which contain sparkling inclusions such as pyrite and biotite, may represent samples the early settlers obtained through trade with the natives.

A wide variety of early seventeenth-century European tobacco pipes were found at 44PG302, along with numerous locally-made pipes, fabricated with varying degrees of sophistication. Archaeologists from VCU found some beautifully decorated Indian trade pipes in a colonial trash pit and some hand-modeled tobacco pipes were unearthed that may have been made by someone of African or Indian origin. A large number of jettons, or "reckoning counters," were found that may have been used in counting, as they often were, or for trade with Native Americans.

Historic Burials at 4PG302

Outside of the fortified compound was a burial ground that ran parallel to the palisade's western and northern walls and contained almost all of the historic period graves associated with 44PG302. Very few of the dead had been buried in coffins and many of the grave shafts were shallow and crudely dug, perhaps because the corpse had been hastily interred. Some of these people had been placed facing east, in accord with Anglican tradition. A surprising number of the burials at 44PG302 were females.

Analysis of the human remains at 44PG302 revealed that more than half of the dead perished between the ages of ten and nineteen and almost a third died while they were in their twenties. Most, if not all, of the burials at 44PG302 were Caucasian, although the race of two children was inconclusive, thanks to bone deterioration. Many of the people interred in the settlement's cemetery showed signs of serious childhood diseases and malnutrition. Those who reached adulthood typically had dental caries and teeth that were worn-down or missing. Few of the individuals who survived into early middle age had teeth. One man, who was between the ages of twenty-five and twenty-nine, may have died as a result of a wound he received at the hands of the Indians, for a small triangular projectile point (Clarksville type) made of quartz was found in association with his remains. This may have been the case, for it is certain that between 1623 and 1625 the natives continued to make sporadic attacks upon the handful of outlying settlements that were strengthened and held. People were mortally wounded at Shirley Hundred, Weyanoke, Martin's Hundred, and other locations that had come under attack in 1622.

Seven of the interments at 44PG302 were situated just outside of the northernmost wall of the palisade, not far from the graves of two women who were placed some twenty-five feet from the settlement's cemetery. Both were white and one, who was between the ages of twenty and twenty-four, was buried in a coffin that had a gable lid. The other, who was between twenty-five and thirty-five, had been placed in a rectangular coffin that was lowered to a depth greater than the other historic burials at 44PG302. A groove in her incisors suggests that she frequently placed a pin in her mouth, perhaps because she was a seamstress. Shroud pins were found in association with the people who had been buried in coffins.

The most elaborate burial unearthed at 44PG302 was a white male likely between thirty-five and thirty-nine years of age, who had been placed in a hexagonal, flat-lidded coffin that was not quite six and a half feet long. His deep, rectangular grave shaft, placed six or seven feet from the north wall of the palisade, had been carefully dug. Numerous coffin nails were found as was two brass plates that may have been the hinges of a document box that perhaps was placed upon the coffin's lid. A fragment of a lock plate also was found in association with this burial. The deceased may have been settlement founder Samuel Jordan, who died in 1623, or perhaps his successor William Farrar, who died around 1637, when he was in his early 40s.

44PG307

Archaeologists from VCU conducted excavations at 44PG307, a domestic complex occupied from the early 1620s to 1635, and discovered that the buildings were enclosed by a simple palisade. There were two large houses and some small ancillary structures that probably were used for agricultural purposes. Structure 10 was eighteen feet wide and just over thirty-six feet in length. It had three bays and may have been laid out in a hall-parlor plan, perhaps with a central passage.

Less than nine feet from Structure 10 was another long, rectangular building, Structure 11. It was identical in size but was placed at a right angle to Structure 10. Archaeologists found evidence of a chimney and hearth and surmised that Structure 11 was the

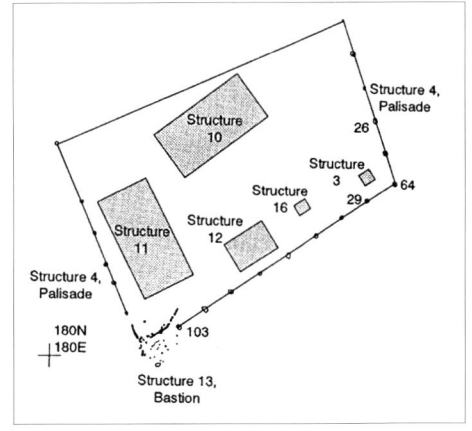

Early seventeenth century cultural features found at 44PG307. Courtesy of Virginia Commonwealth University.

principal dwelling house at 44PG307. Although archaeologists found many parallels between the fortified domestic complex at 44PG307 and the one at 44PG302 (the probable Jordan-Farrar site), the artifacts recovered from 44PG307 suggest

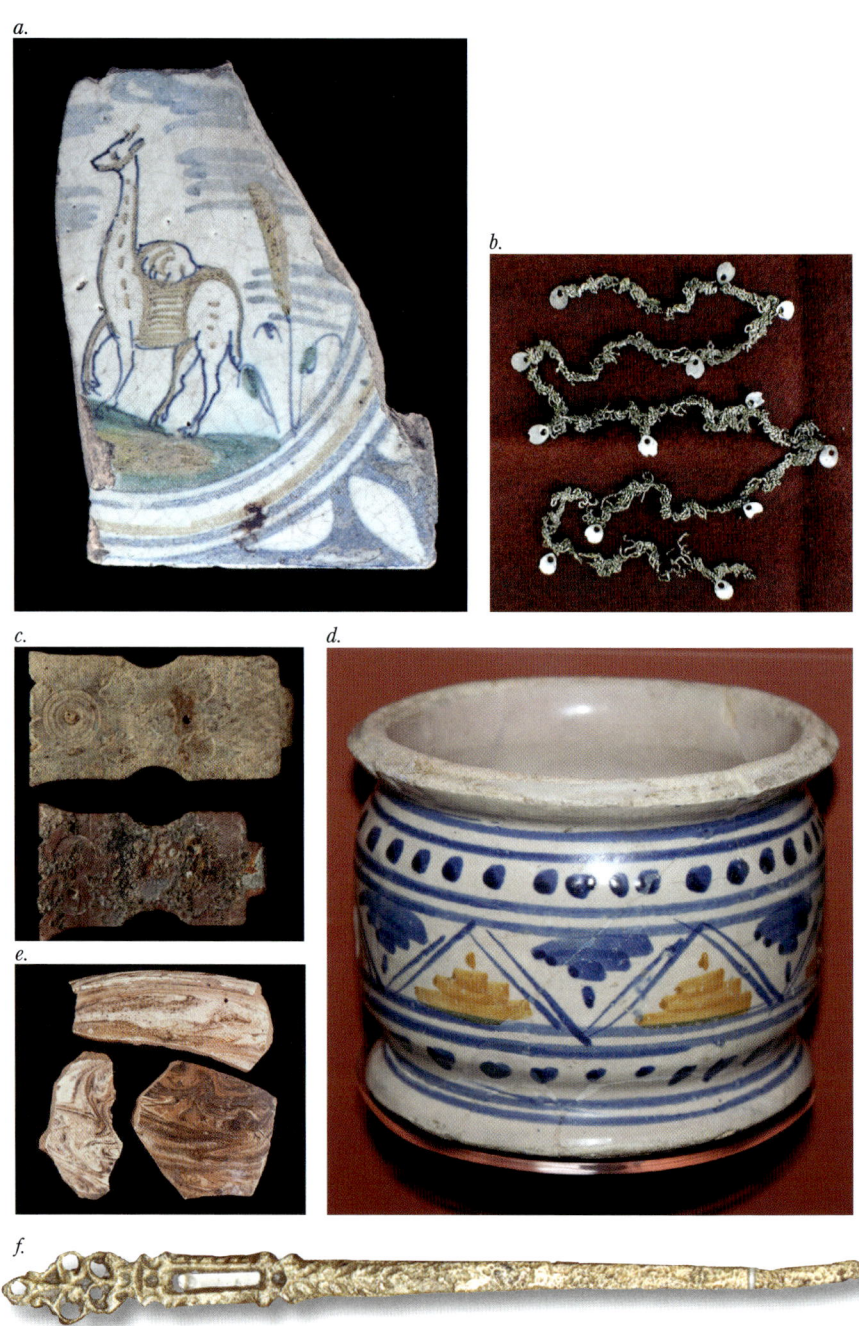

Artifacts found at 44PG307: a. Tin-enameled earthenware tile, Courtesy of Virginia Common-wealth University; b. Silver embroidery, VDHR photo; c. Brass book hinges or clasps, Courtesy of Virginia Commonwealth University; d. Tin-enameled earthenware ointment pot, Courtesy of Virginia Commonwealth University; e. North Italian marbleized polychrome slipware, Courtesy of Virginia Commonwealth University, f. Brass bodkin, VDHR photo.

that the people who lived there were of somewhat lesser means. For example, the lady of the house tucked a brass bodkin into her hair rather than one fabricated of silver, and one of the male residents wore clothing that was decorated with copper threads rather than gold.

The substantial quantity of fragments of upscale ceramics and other refined household accoutrements at 44PG307 prompted curator Taft Kiser to raise the possibility that Nathaniel Causey and his wife occupied the site, which was directly across the James River from their plantation, Causey's Care. Kiser noted that the ceramics found at 44PG307, which were from the vicinity of London, were of comparable quality to those at 44PG302 but were somewhat brighter, even gaudy. For example, at 44PG307, the fireplace was rimmed with brightly colored polychrome tiles, but at 44PG302 the main fireplace was adorned with worked fragments of calcareous stone. Kiser concluded that the Causeys, whose socioeconomic standing was comparable to that of William and Cisley Jordan Farrar, probably lived at 44PG307 and made a substantial investment in their household furnishings.

Nathaniel Causey, a burgess for Jordan's Journey in 1624, was entrusted with goods that belonged to the Truelove's Company, items that would have come into his possession around 1625. On the other hand, Causey made a trip to London during the late 1620s and may have purchased new tableware and other "modern" items he found appealing. Archaeologists found evidence of two buildings at 44PG307, the same number of houses attributed to Nathaniel Causey in 1625. If he resided at the site, which was on Jordan's Point's northeastern face, he would have had an unobstructed view of his own property, directly across the James. He also would have had a vantage point that would have allowed him to see down the James River. The stem of a brass candlestick was found at 44PG307 as were firedogs with brass finials. Also recovered were brass book hasps, which suggest that one or more of the site's occupants were literate.

44PG151

In 1987 archaeologists from the JRIA conducted excavations at 44PG151, where they found evidence of at least two phases of historic occupation. The first period, which dated to 1620–1640, was associated with the loosely defined community known as Jordan's Journey. Archaeologists uncovered an earthfast building that measured eighteen feet by twenty feet and had been constructed with preassembled side walls. They also found evidence suggesting that a wood-and-clay chimney had been located at the northeast corner of the house. Fragments of locally-made pipes found in several post molds suggest a post-1625 destruction date.

Early seventeenth-century ceramics found in association with 44PG151 included fragments of Dutch or Anglo-Netherlandish delftware tile, the base of a Westerwald stoneware jug, the base of a Rhenish stoneware jug, and a sherd of a coarseware porringer made by an artisan working at Jamestown during the 1630s, perhaps an apprentice of Martin's Hundred potter Thomas Ward. Two pieces of Frechen brown stoneware also were found. An iron fireplace shovel, an iron hammer, a snaphaunce trigger guard, and a brass jetton were recovered from 44PG151 along with an early seventeenth-century brass skillet and Wolf Laufer jettons (1618-1660). Brass straight pins, a brass clothing fastener, and an iron drawer pull attest to the domestic nature of the site. A large quantity of prehistoric pottery also was found at 44PG151, along with one Native American burial.

The presence of only one building and a scarcity of artifacts suggest that 44PG151 had few occupants. It may be significant that in 1625 nine households at Jordan's Journey had only one house and that only two of those nine were occupied by one person, a man. This raises the possibility that 44PG151 was occupied by Joseph Bull or Thomas Causey, both of whom lived alone. Bull came to Virginia in the *Abigail* in 1622. As his name was omitted from the census made in 1624, his whereabouts are unknown prior to early 1625. He then had some stored food, lead shot, a firearm, a coat of chain mail, and a protective headpiece, which suggest that he was well prepared for life in the colony. Bull also had a few poultry.

On the other hand, Thomas Causey, who had arrived in the *Francis Bonaventure* in 1620 and had been living at Hog Island in February 1624 and in early 1625, would have been a relative newcomer to Jordan's Journey. In January 1625 he was credited with one house but had neither servants nor live-stock. Like Joseph Bull, Thomas Causey had a supply of stored food, defensive weaponry, and some poultry. Although the relationship between Thomas and Nathaniel Causey is unclear, they probably were kinsman. If so, Thomas may have purposefully settled at 44PG151, in close proximity to 44PG307, where Nathaniel probably was living.

44PG300

Archaeologist James G. Harrison, III, who undertook excavations at 44PG300, concluded that it was occupied around the same time as 44PG302, the probable home of the Jordan-Farrar household. Site 44PG300 is located on the northeast side of Jordan's Point, somewhat inland from the large headland's tip. The three-bay dwelling found at 44PG300 measured twenty-nine feet by nineteen feet and probably was occupied from the early 1620s until around 1640. Archaeologists determined that it was more sturdily constructed than most earthfast structures that date to the second quarter of the seventeenth century, for studs had been placed between the principal posts. At the end of the building were traces of a probable wattle fence. Substantial concentrations of artifacts and the presence of eleven early seventeenth-century burials suggest that 44PG300 was occupied by a relatively large group of people who lived communally. The presence of silver threads, Roemer glass, and porcelain suggests that the site was home to people of superior social status. A silver cosmetic implement found at 44PG300 probably functioned as a combination ear scoop and nail or tooth cleaner. It has a loop and silver ring that would have enabled its owner to suspend it from a chatelaine.

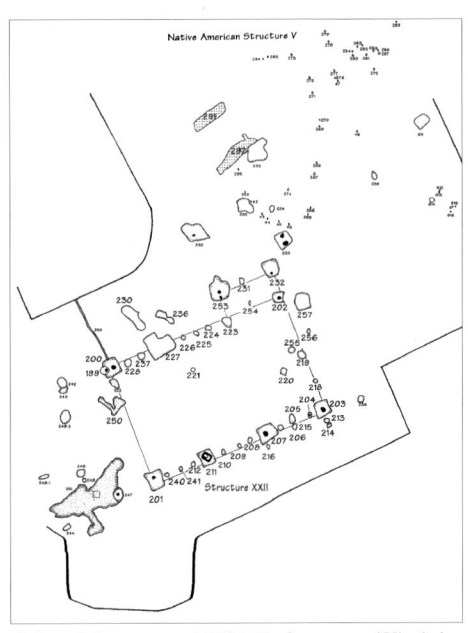

Cultural features at 44PG300. Courtesy of Virginia Company after James G. Harrison, III.

Site 44PG300 most likely was occupied by the relatively large group of refugees from Berkeley Hundred, at least eleven men, women, and children who permanently abandoned their original settlement and stayed on at Jordan's Journey. Among them were Thomas Palmer, Richard Milton, and John Gibbs, all of whom were prominent gentlemen. An additional sixteen people who left Berkeley Hundred after the 1622 Indian attack also may have gone to Jordan's Journey. A latten seal-top spoon found at 44PG300, incised with an "X," matched one that was found at 44PG302 and may have belonged to tailor Christopher Bourton, who survived the Indian attack upon Berkeley Hundred. On the beach, about fifty feet from the dwelling at 44PG300, was a barrel well, near which was found an early seventeenth-century tobacco pipe bearing the initials WI. Decorative brass finials that once adorned a set of fireplace tongs and a pair of lead gaming dice, perhaps fabricated from discarded lead, were found at 44PG300.

Tools were found in abundance at 44PG300, notably broad hoes and hilling hoes, felling axes, and a broad axe that would have been useful for hewing or squaring timber. A sickle recovered had a serrated edge, that would have allowed its user to cut hay or grasses with a quick flick of the wrist. The two augers and a claw-type hammer that were found would have been used by someone working in wood. They may have belonged to Richard Sheriffe and his son, two of the carpenters and coopers the Society of Berkeley Hundred's investors sent to Virginia.

Two breastplates and four back plates were unearthed at 44PG300 along with other pieces of military attire. Pieces of a brigandine, a close-fitting coat comprised of thin, narrow iron plates riveted to strong, coarse cloth, were found at the site. A brigandine's outer surface often was covered with velvet or another fine fabric that rendered it suitable for wear on special occasions. Chain mail, a

Artifacts found at 44PG300: a. Peascod breastplate. VDHR photo.; b. Sickle. Drawing by Jamie May, VDHR photo.; c. Roemer glass.; d. A porcelain wine cup, ca. 1613. A blue underglaze frieze of flames embellishes the exterior. Courtesy of Virginia Commonwealth University; e. Portion of a Portuguese majolica caudle cup. VDHR photo.; f. Donyatt South Somerset, U.K. wet sgraffito slipware. Courtesy of Virginia Commonwealth University; g. Silver cosmetic implement. Drawing by Jamie May, VDHR photo.

type of protective metal fabric, was found. It was composed of interlocking rings and was a type of flexible "armor" that offered protection against knives and swords but was ineffective against spears and other projectiles. Tasset lames, plates that would have hung from the lower part of a breastplate, were found at 44PG300, as were sword hilts. In early 1625 Thomas Palmer was credited with three sets of armor and a coat of chain mail and Richard Milton had armor. Both men, who had been associated with Berkeley Hundred, had stores of firearms, shot, and powder. Their weaponry may have been part of the military supplies sent to Virginia in the wake of the 1622 Indian attack.

Fragments of at least 149 early seventeenth-century ceramic vessels were recovered from 44PG300. The overwhelming majority were earthenware vessels from England, Holland, Portugal, Spain, and Germany that were used for food preparation and storage. Stoneware from England and Germany made up twenty-two percent of the total. Vessels used for the serving and consumption of beverages and food were numerous. They included wine glasses embellished with prunts, small rounds of glass that often were applied to stemware. They were decorative but served a practical purpose, for people ate with their hands and prunts kept glass vessels from slipping through greasy fingers.

Sherds of a Portuguese majolica caudal cup were found at 44PG300 as were pieces of several delftware drug jars, chargers, plates, and dishes. Nearly half of the ceramic vessel fragments recovered were from Dutch, Spanish, Portuguese, and English coarsewares along with pottery produced at Jamestown. They included pieces of storage jars, milk pans, and cooking vessels. Remnants of Iberian olive storage jars and Spanish earthenware costrels also were present along with Rhenish blue and gray stoneware jugs and Rhenish brown stoneware.

Relatively few of the ceramic vessel fragments found at 44PG300 were associated with food consumption, perhaps because the site's occupants, like others of elevated social status, used pewter plates, pieces of which rarely are recovered during archaeological excavations. One artifact suggesting an association with the elite was a Chinese export porcelain wine cup that dates to the first quarter of the seventeenth century and would have been rare in its day.

Taft Kiser noted that although very similar ceramics were recovered from all of the early-seventeenth-century sites at Jordan's Point, 44PG300 had an especially generous selection of South Somerset slipwares, which were present in great abundance. That led him to surmise that the site's occupants were recent arrivals from England, possibly from the Bristol area. Significantly, most of the Society of Berkeley Hundred's settlers disembarked from Bristol, in southwestern England, and the Society's principal investors were based in Gloucestershire, near Bristol.

The inventory of Berkeley Hundred leader George Thorpe, who was slain by attacking Indians in March 1622, reveals much about the types of material goods the Society of Berkeley Hundred's settlers brought to Virginia. In

Thorpe's possession at the time of his death were two pewter porringers, six small porcelain dishes, a gilt bowl, a silver cup, five silver spoons, and a pair of knives and a spoon that had gilt handles. Thorpe also had a brass baking pan, a large brass pot, several pie plates, platters and saucers, and a generous supply of clothing. His household furnishings included bedding, three large chests, curtains, feather beds, and two clothes cupboards. Also present were utilitarian items such as a copper still, tools, fish hooks, sea compasses, and a quadrant.

The Society of Berkeley Hundred's settlers, who were sent to Virginia in groups and chosen on account of their specialized skills, were expected to lead a communal lifestyle. When the first contingent arrived, they were supposed to build a sturdily framed storehouse to hold their food supply, tools, and weapons, and a hall where they could dine and gather for meetings and worship. Households were to erect "homelike" board-covered shelters. The Berkeley Hundred community's leadership, like that of other particular plantations, was supposed to consist of a commander and a handful of lesser officials. Although the 1622 Indian attack undoubtedly caused chaos, it is likely that Berkeley Hundred's surviving leaders quickly tried to reestablish order. Upon withdrawing to Jordan's Journey, they may have opted to resume the communal lifestyle to which they had become accustomed at Berkeley Hundred. This mode of living would have contrasted sharply with that of the other, more independent planter households at Jordan's Journey.

HISTORIC BURIALS AT 44PG300

Dr. Douglas Owsley, who examined the human burials at 44PG300, determined that there were five females, two males, and four individuals whose gender could not be determined. At least one of the people interred at 44PG300 was buried in a gable-lidded coffin, which suggests that he was a higher status individual. He was a very large man, who died when he was twenty-five to thirty-five years old. He was crowded into a six-foot-long hexagonal coffin that was oriented on an east-west axis, in accord with Christian burial practices. The lower part of his left leg was missing just below the knee cap, a loss that probably occurred before his death and hastened it. This raises the possibility that the man was injured during the 1622 Indian attack and was buried at Jordan's Journey. According to Captain John Smith, the natives mutilated at least one corpse, that of George Thorpe.

Another person buried in a coffin was a woman who perished when she was between the ages of sixteen and twenty-two. Dr. Owsley identified her as Caucasian, but noted that the shape of her teeth suggested that she may have had some Native American ancestry. Also found at 44PG300 were the graves of two young girls, one of whom appears to have been hastily interred. Two other burials may be those of a mother and infant. Among the other interments at Jordan's Point was a woman who died when she was between the ages of twenty and twenty-four. She was buried in clothing that was adorned with buttons containing silver thread, evidence of her superior social status. A horizontal line of stain below her pelvis suggests that she may have been wearing a long vest-like garment at the time of burial.

The remains of a white man, who was between thirty-five and forty-five at the time of his death, also were found. Just below his lower jaw, excavators found traces of material that had been stitched with silver thread, perhaps the remains of a collar. A line of staining below the man's pelvis suggests that he was buried in a doublet, a close-fitting jacket worn by males of high socioeconomic status. The decedent may have been John Gibbs, one of three prominent men from Bermuda Hundred who moved to Jordan's Journey after the 1622 Indian attack. Although Thomas Palmer and Richard Milton went elsewhere, in 1632 John Gibbs was still associated with the Society of Berkeley Hundred and asked its investors to consider reviving their plantation. Prehistoric and historic artifacts intruded upon most of the historic burials found at 44PG300, probably when the grave shafts were backfilled.

The historic period burials at 44PG300 were clustered in three groups and shared a common orientation. The average age at death ranged from nineteen to twenty-six years. One of the burials at 44PG300 showed evidence of broad band hypoplasia, a condition produced by severe nutritional stress during growth periods. Fully eighty percent of the burial population showed evidence of childhood exposure to malnutrition or disease, typically between the ages of three and four years old.

WHAT'S FOR DINNER?

In 1996 Dr. Joanne Bowen of the Colonial Williamsburg Foundation studied the faunal remains excavated from the early seventeenth century historic sites at Jordan's Point. She found that during the first few decades of settlement, wildlife made up anywhere from nine percent to forty percent of the total meat consumed. The early faunal assemblages at Jordan's Point reveal that the occupants of 44PG302, 44PG307, 44PG300, and 44PG151 followed a slightly different pattern of meat consumption than occurred elsewhere in the Chesapeake. According to Henry Miller, who studied meat consumption patterns in several early Chesapeake settlements, hogs and cattle flourished in the region and soon provided the bulk of the colonists' meat. He concluded that pork usually was consumed in almost equal proportion to beef. Historical accounts reveal that swine were able to thrive when allowed to forage in the forests, for they ate almost anything, bred prolifically, and were ferocious enough to fend off predators. Cattle also were able to flourish for they foraged in meadows, wetlands, and forests. Palisades and other enclosures provided cattle with a measure of protection as did islands and peninsulas.

The meat diet of those who lived at 44PG302, likely the home of William and Cisley Jordan Farrar, consisted of roughly forty-six percent beef, twelve percent pork, three percent mutton or goat meat, and just over seven percent venison. Thus, domestic livestock provided most of the meat that graced the household's dinner table. On the other hand, those who lived at 44PG307, perhaps Nathaniel Causey and his family, ate more than four times as much venison and seemingly, neither mutton nor goat meat. The occupants of 44PG151 frequently dined upon beef and pork but also consumed meat supplied by sheep or goats.

Significantly, the occupants of 44PG300 relied more heavily upon beef than pork but supplemented their diet with venison. They probably were people sent over by the Society of Berkeley Hundred, who in September 1619 instructed its first settlers to enclose 400 acres of grazing land with a strong palisade as pasturage for their livestock. After the 1622 Indian attack, Berkeley Hundred's cattle were carefully preserved. Some were placed at Flowerdew Hundred and some at Shirley Hundred. The purposeful husbandry of the Society of Berkeley Hundred's cattle may explain the preponderance of beef at 44PG300.

Jordan's Journey's early inhabitants' table fare included numerous types of meat and seafood. They consumed a variety of wild fowl (such as ducks, geese, loons, herons, cormorants, swans, rails, and gulls), turtles, wild mammals (such as rabbits, opossum, muskrats, bears, deer, and raccoons) and local fish. Fish were present in all of the early seventeenth century faunal assemblages at Jordan's Point, but were not as important a food source as usually is presumed. Seafood accounted for less than one percent of the assemblages from 44PG300 and 44PG307, but for eight and a half percent in 44PG302. Among the types of fish consumed were gars, eels, herrings, suckers, catfish, pickerels, cod, haddock, perches, bluegills, and drums.

Remarkably, substantial quantities of the fish consumed at 44PG302 were imported haddock and Atlantic cod, cold water species that the New England fisheries sold commercially. During the colonial period, Atlantic cod was salted so that it could be preserved and haddock was packed in brine and brought to Virginia in barrels, a type of storage vessel mentioned in the 1625 muster. Because provisions were in such short supply right after the 1622 Indian attack, the Privy Council and certain merchants sent ships to the colony with large quantities of fish that had been obtained from Canada and Newfoundland. One shipment contained 40,000 fish. In November 1622, John Farrar, a kinsman of William Farrar of Jordan's Journey, was authorized to send a group of people to Virginia where he also was allowed to sell fish. This may explain the preponderance of imported haddock and cod at 44PG302.

Through the analysis of faunal materials, Dr. Joanne Bowen found that wild birds made up almost five percent of the total assemblage from 44PG300, but only a little over one percent at 44PG302, and the occupants of 44PG307 consumed even less. Bones from ducks, geese, turkeys, rails, and bobwhites were present, wild fowl still considered good eating, but some less appealing fowl were consumed, notably pelican, swan, horned grebe, loons, egret, and cormorant. Deer comprised just over thirty-two percent of the early assemblage from 44PG307, whose occupants may have traded with the Indians or hired them to hunt. Considerably less venison was eaten at 44PG302 and 44PG300.

Besides meat, Virginia's colonists consumed fruit and vegetables. Early writers commented upon the abundance of edible berries and nuts and at Jamestown and outlying plantations, settlers planted vegetable gardens, grape vines, and fruit trees. The colonists were required to grow corn (maize) which could be dried and stored, and they availed themselves of other crops like peas, beans, and squash that the natives grew. The 1625 muster, which lists the supply of stored food at Jordan's Journey, demonstrates how important it was to preserve provisions for leaner times. Incoming ships brought oatmeal, cheese, butter, prunes, alcoholic beverages, and other consumables. The consumption of wine, cider, or beer also was an essential part of a colonist's table fare.

THE DEMISE OF JORDAN'S JOURNEY

Archaeological evidence suggests that by 1640 the sites that European colonists developed at Jordan's Journey during the early 1620s had been abandoned. By that time, the settlement's commander, William Farrar, was dead and most of the community's other inhabitants had died or moved to property of their own. For example, John Flood moved to nearby Westover and then went to Surry County, and Henry Williams patented land on the Eastern Shore. William Farrar's sons, on the other hand, took up residence in the newly formed Henrico County. But Jordan's Point, a highly desirable piece of real estate, became an important plantation and family seat.

King Charles II. Courtesy of the Colonial Williamsburg Foundation.

CHAPTER 6

The Context of Settlement

THE INSTITUTION OF LOCAL GOVERNMENT

By 1634, there were 4,914 European colonists in Virginia, 511 of whom lived between Shirley Hundred (Eppes) Island and Weyanoke, the territory in which Jordan's Point is located. Because population growth was accompanied by a burgeoning number of court cases, the governor and his council, who functioned as a judiciary body, quickly found their workload burdensome. Therefore, to free the colony's highest ranking officials from settling petty disputes and dealing with other routine matters, the assembly decided to subdivide Virginia into eight shires or counties. Each of the newly formed counties had a court and justices, one of whom had to be a council member. William Farrar of Jordan's Journey, a member of the Council of State, was qualified to serve in that capacity and hosted court sessions in his home.

Charles City County was vast and spanned both sides of the James River. On the upper side of the James, Charles City's boundaries ran in a westerly direction from a point just above the Chickahominy River's mouth to the western limits of West and Shirley Hundred. On the lower side of the James, the county ran from Upper Chippokes Creek (on the east) to the mouth of the Appomattox River (on the west).

Provisions were made for each county to have a sheriff and a military commander or lieutenant, who was responsible for organizing and maintaining the local militia. During the decade that followed, county court justices became responsible for seeing that public graveyards were laid out and enclosed; that roads, bridges and ferries were maintained; and that taverns and mills operated within the law. They also were authorized to try most civil cases, probate wills, collect taxes, and to distribute arms and ammunition to the local militia. By 1652 county courts had jurisdiction over most local affairs.

Scholars agree that the rise of representative government in Virginia occurred incrementally, thanks to the Crown's failure to interfere in the manner in which it was evolving. The colony's assembly, through trial and error, gradually acquired some fundamental rights, at times gaining more power than its counterpart enjoyed in England. By 1643 Virginia's Grand Assembly had become bicameral, for the burgesses convened apart from the governor and council. Both bodies worked closely with local officials in solving whatever problems arose. Virginia's legal system was based upon English law. Special legislation was enacted from time to time to meet the colony's changing needs.

CLASS DIFFERENCES EMERGE

As the seventeenth century wore on and the colony's population increased, social and political distinctions between the classes became more apparent and Virginia became a distinctly stratified society. Servants fulfilled their terms of indenture and often sought to procure land of their own, but lacked the means to do so. This led to a growing number of landless freedmen who leased land from larger planters or simply became transients. At the pinnacle of Virginia society were the governor and his councilors, who held the colony's top posts and shared some of their power with members of the assembly. Below the burgesses were county justices of the peace and other local officials. At the bottom were the lesser planters and landless freedmen who ranked just above ethnic minorities, such as blacks and Indians, whose legal rights and opportunities for advancement were diminishing. Somewhere between the top and bottom rungs of the socioeconomic ladder were the Virginians whose landholdings were of modest size. These were the middling farmers, skilled workers, and others with a limited but adequate amount of disposable income.

ECONOMIC PROGRESS

In March 1631 Governor John Harvey and his council, who were eager to strengthen the colony's economic position, informed British officials that tradesmen (such as shipwrights, smiths, carpenters, tanners, and other skilled workers, especially those who made and laid brick) were urgently needed. By 1633 there were five tobacco inspection warehouses in the colony, one of which was at Eppes Island, just west of Jordan's Point and almost directly across the river. During the 1630s commerce was brisk between the colonists of Virginia and New Amsterdam (New York). Twice during the 1640s, when Sir William Berkeley was governor, the Dutch were invited to trade in Virginia. Such commerce was a long-standing tradition and the Dutch apparently welcomed the opportunity to trade freely and openly. In 1648 one man commented that "At last Christmas we had trading here [at Jamestown] ten ships from London, two from Bristoll, twelve Hollanders, and seven from New England." A navigation act imposed by the English government at mid-century, which forbade the importation of goods in foreign ships, was enormously unpopular.

Despite growth in the colony's population and the expansion of settlement into new territory, the old ruling families and their kin clung tightly to their power and dominated Virginia's government. Their ranks were increased by new arrivals who came with money and good political connections. By the mid-seventeenth century, settlement was well established throughout Tidewater Virginia, east of the fall line, and across the Chesapeake Bay on the Eastern Shore. The mortality rate began to level off and by 1649 Virginia had an estimated 5,000 inhabitants of European origin. The colony not only had managed to survive, it was gaining in momentum.

INTERACTION WITH THE NATIVES

Although the early 1630s were marked by sporadic Indian attacks and regular retaliatory expeditions, a great drought in the summer of 1632 shriveled the corn crop and forced the colonists to initiate trade with the natives. A tenuous peace agreement was made with the Chickahominys and Pamunkeys in October, although they were still considered "Irreconcilable enemies" who were not to be trusted. Undoubtedly, the relentless spread of European settlement, which was extending inland at a relatively rapid rate, increased tensions. Laws were made whereby no imported cloth, cotton, or other goods could be traded with the Indians and nobody was to parley with any natives except those of the Eastern Shore. Any Indian the colonists encountered was to be brought to the nearest commander.

Selling firearms to the Indians was strictly illegal but in 1637 sanctions against other types of trade were lifted. There was considerable cultural contact between the Indians and the colonists during this period and some natives became servants in planters' homes. This antagonized tribal leaders, who complained about a shortage of workers. Settlers were encouraged to take Indian children into their homes and rear them in the Christian faith. In 1641 Walter Aston of nearby Causey's Care in Charles City County was one of four men granted the right to explore the territory beyond the head of the Appomattox River. They hoped to establish trade with the Indians and to discover potentially marketable commodities.

THE IMPACT OF POPULATION GROWTH

Although the colonists and Indians made a new peace agreement in April 1642, Virginia planters' relentless intrusion into native lands inevitably gave rise to conflict. On April 18, 1644, some of the tribes of the Powhatan Chiefdom again united in a concerted attempt to drive the European colonists from their homeland. This second major Indian attack claimed between 400 and 500 settlers' lives. Especially hard hit were the upper reaches of the York River and the territory on the south side of the James, near its mouth. Opechancanough, who had

Sir William Berkeley, Virginia's governor. The Jamestown-Yorktown Collection, Williamsburg, Va. USA.

led the 1622 attack, was credited with leading the second one. A charismatic leader who was greatly revered, he was said to be almost one hundred years old.

The Grand Assembly responded to the Indian attack by resolving to destroy all natives they believed had had a hand in the bloodshed. In July 1644 marches were undertaken against the Weyanoke, Pamunkey, Warresqueak, and Nansemond Indians, along with some tribes that lived within what eventually became North Carolina. The colonists continued to embark upon retaliatory expeditions, just as they had in 1622, but the Indians simply faded into the forest and then dropped out of sight. Because of the critical shortage of ammunition, the assembly fixed upon a strategy that required fewer armed men—building forts or surveillance posts on the fringes of the colony's frontier. In February 1645 Secretary Richard Kemp informed Governor William Berkeley that if the Indians had realized how little powder and shot the colonists had, they would have been in great jeopardy.

A search party was sent out to capture Opechancanough, dead or alive. Governor William Berkeley, upon learning that the aged chief's people had been sighted, rallied a party of armed horsemen and apprehended him. While he was incarcerated at Jamestown, a soldier shot him in the back. The death of the natives' paramount leader heralded the Powhatan Chiefdom's demise and reputedly made Governor Berkeley the "darling of the people."

THE 1646 TREATY

In October 1646, a treaty was signed by Necotowance, "Emperor of the Indians" and Opechancanough's immediate successor, who represented several native groups formerly unified under the revered paramount chief. This landmark peace agreement forced the native people to make several important sacrifices.

Under the terms of the treaty, the Indians relinquished their land rights, acknowledging that possession of their territory was at the behest of the English monarch. Thus, they formally became tributaries to the Crown. The imposition of a tributary system, not unlike the manner in which Powhatan and then Opechancanough had ruled the tribes under their control, was in fact a tangible symbol of the Indians' political subservience to the English.

The Tributary Indians agreed to let Virginia's governor appoint or confirm their leaders. This was an especially important concession, for it hastened the disintegration of the Powhatan Chiefdom by scattering the native groups tradi-

The elderly paramount chief Opechancanough, slain at Jamestown while in captivity. Courtesy of the National Park Service, Colonial National Historical Park, Jamestown Collection.

tionally unified under a powerful paramount leader. As one government official put it, Governor Berkeley and his council believed that a "divide and conquer" approach was the most expedient way to reduce the Indians into subservience.

In accord with the 1646 treaty, the Indians agreed to vacate the territory on the lower side of the James River, southward to the Blackwater River, and on the James-York peninsula inland to the fall line. In return, the Virginia government agreed to protect the Indians from their enemies and to restrict European settlement to the ceded territory. The only natives allowed to enter the area reserved to the colonists' use were official messengers who had to be clad in special striped coats that could be obtained from one of the frontier forts established in 1645-1646. Colonists living on the lower side of the James River were obliged to conduct all Indian trade at Fort Henry on the Appomattox River. That would have been the trading post nearest the colonists living in the vicinity of Jordan's Point.

Despite the terms of the 1646 treaty, within three years settlement was allowed to expand into the territory formerly reserved to the natives' use. The policy change occurred in sync with the official abandonment of the military outposts established in 1645 and 1646. During the 1640s and 50s, "seating" (settlement) requirements were extremely lax, and under the law only one house had to be built and one acre of ground placed under cultivation to substantiate a new land claim.

In October 1649 land was assigned to three Indian kings, at their request. Ascomowett, king of the Weyanoke, then received 5,000 acres of land on the lower side of the James River at Warreko. The natives again acknowledged that the land they were receiving belonged to the English monarch. The assembly, in turn, agreed that the Indians had the right to keep the land then in their possession and forbade settlers from encroaching upon their territory. The burgesses also acknowledged that taking the Indians' lands often had driven them to a desperate course of action. The establishment of tribal lands or preserves, which dispersed the natives into small, clustered groups, quickly became policy. The natives' ranks continued to dwindle and in 1669 the Weyanoke were said to have only fifteen warriors, then living in Surry County.

As racial tensions eased, Virginia colonists and their Indian neighbors again began to intermingle. However, land-hungry planters paid little heed to native rights and brazenly seated themselves on the Indians' property or tried to trick them into selling it. Also, the natives' population diminished and that of the colonists surged. This put increased pressure upon the Indians, whose hunting and foraging habitat gradually was reduced.

THE CIVIL WAR IN ENGLAND

Even before England became embroiled in a bloody civil war, tensions between the Royalists (the monarchy's supporters) and the Roundheads (those

Courtesy of the Library of Congress.

who backed Parliament) spilled over onto the colonies. Many Virginians were sympathetic to the monarchy and in 1649, when King Charles I was beheaded, the assembly proclaimed his son's right to the throne and declared it treasonous to question Charles II's right of succession. Governor William Berkeley, who was fiercely loyal to the Crown, opened his home to Royalists seeking refuge in Virginia.

After the war in England came to an end and Oliver Cromwell became Protector of the Commonwealth, a Parliamentary fleet set sail for Virginia to assert its authority over a colony known as a Royalist stronghold. In April 1652 Sir William Berkeley, who had governed Virginia since 1641, was obliged to surrender the colony and relinquish his office. The colonists also had to hand over all publicly-owned arms and ammunition. The assembly could conduct business as usual as long as its laws were in keeping with those of the Commonwealth and the colony's charter and the legality of its land patents were to be upheld. Virginians had the right to free trade and no taxes, customs or imposts could be imposed upon them without their assembly's consent. During the Interregnum, settlement continued to fan out in every direction as forested lands yielded to the axe and became cleared fields that were converted to agriculture. Tidewater Virginia was dotted with small and middling farmsteads that were interspersed with the larger plantations of the well-to-do, who typically monopolized local political power.

THE NATIVES AS TRIBUTARIES

During the early-to-mid 1650s Virginia's tributary Indians commenced making use of the colony's legal system and occasionally served as military allies. In March 1656 Pamunkey and Chickahominy warriors assisted the colonists in driving off 600 to 700 hostile natives who had descended upon homesteads near the falls of the James River. This conflict-turned-tragedy, the Battle of Bloody Run, claimed the life of the Pamunkey Indian leader, Totopotomoy. Later in the year, laws were enacted that required Indians to carry a pass or ticket whenever they wanted to hunt, fish or forage within the colonized area. A 1662 law forced them to wear silver or copper badges, inscribed with their tribe's name, whenever they entered the territory inhabited by the colonists. Special markets for Indian trade were established in certain counties.

BENJAMIN SIDDWAY (SIDWAY) AND THE BLANDS

By the 1640s or the early 1650s, the late Samuel Jordan's property at Jordan's Point in Charles City County had come into the hands of Captain Benjamin Siddway (Sidway) and his wife, Mary. She was the widow of Benjamin Harrison II, whose plantation, Wakefield, was on the east side of Upper Chippokes Creek, where Benjamin Siddway also owned land.

By the 1640s, Benjamin Siddway had begun having business dealings with John Bland, a prominent London merchant who was actively engaged in transatlantic commerce. For example, in 1644 Bland's ship, the *Civil Merchant*, sailed from London to Bermuda, and then continued on to Virginia. After tobacco was loaded aboard, the vessel went to Cadiz, in Spain, and then set out for Barbados and Virginia. A list of the goods John Bland sent to Virginia on another ship reveals that his cargo, which was offloaded at Jamestown, the official port of entry, included everything from household goods and clothing to ammunition, tools and alcoholic beverages. Bland also sent indentured servants to the colony, where there was a labor shortage. In 1644 John Bland's brother, Adam, served as his factor or business representative aboard the ship, but another brother, Edward, was his factor in Virginia.

In 1647 Edward Bland patented land near the head of Upper Chippokes Creek, to the east of Jordan's Point, and became one of Benjamin Siddway's trading partners. Court testimony taken in 1653 indicates that in 1649 John Bland dispatched his ship, the *Virginia Merchant*, from Gravesend, England, with goods that were consigned to Benjamin Siddway, Edward Bland, and Richard Bland, then in Virginia and serving as his agents. A quantity of wine was put aboard the ship along with some lead that Edward Bland planned to have made into gutters for his house.

Besides his involvement in transatlantic commerce, Edward Bland was keenly interested in Indian trade. On August 27, 1650, he set out from Fort Henry with Abraham Wood, Sackford Brewster, and Elias Pennant on an exploratory journey into the territory at the head of Appomattox River. Oyeocker, a Nottoway Indian leader, and Pyancha, an Appomattock Indian war captain, served as guides. During the men's journey into the land they called "New Britaine," they visited several Indian towns, encountering the Weyanoke, Meherrin, Tuscarora, and other native groups. Bland and his traveling companions hoped to open the area to settlement and to establish a trading monopoly.

After Edward Bland's death around 1651, Benjamin Siddway continued to trade with London merchant John Bland and probably served as his mercantile firm's factor in the upper reaches of the James River. Siddway worked closely with Captain William Rothwell, his agent or tenant at Jordan's Point, and he also had dealings with John Richards of London, who had settled in Virginia and become a merchant. In 1652 when Surry County was formed, Benjamin Siddway, a resident of Southwark Parish, became a county justice and militia officer, an indication of his status in the community. However, shortly thereafter he began having serious financial problems, some of which may have been attributable to a new trade policy that was adopted by Virginia's legislators.

THE ESTABLISHMENT OF COUNTY MARKETS

In March 1653 the assembly created special trading zones. Each of Virginia's counties was authorized to establish one or two markets that extended for a mile or so along both sides of a major navigable waterway. The markets,

which had to be at least ten miles apart, served as an official port of entry through which all foreign vessels had to pass when unlading goods, merchandise, and servants that were to be offered for sale. Incoming merchants and traders were to provide the market's clerk with an inventory of all cargo that was to be offloaded. Merchandise that had been for sale at an official market for eight months or more could be taken

An English tobacco label. Courtesy of the Imperial Tobacco Company.

elsewhere and sold. Although the establishment of county markets undoubtedly put small traders and middlemen at a significant disadvantage, the new policy gave inhabitants of outlying settlements immediate access to newly imported goods and servants, which previously had to pass through Jamestown, the sole port of entry.

The justices of Charles City and Surry Counties responded to the passage of the act by designating Westover and Martin's Brandon as their official markets. The trading zone extended along the banks of the James River for two miles and all imported goods and servants were to be brought ashore there. Each market had a clerk who was supposed to maintain accurate accounts of all imports that entered his area and make note of any goods or servants that were transferred to another trading site. Howell Pryse (Price) was the market clerk at Westover.

It is likely that when Westover, then owned by Sir John Pawlett, and Martin's Brandon, which belonged to a group of merchants, became county markets, any trading activities that formerly occurred at Jordan's Point were greatly reduced or perhaps curtailed altogether. In fact, merchant-trader Captain William Rothwell of Jordan's Point and his successor, George Potter, probably had to sell their goods at Westover, the market nearest their base of operations, and wait the obligatory eight months before they could transfer leftover imported goods to Jordan's Point.

This change in trading practices may have been Benjamin Siddway's undoing. By the time the act creating county markets was repealed, he was deeply indebted to John and Theodorick Bland, his employers. On September 4, 1657, Benjamin Siddway and his wife Mary transferred to the Blands "a Certain parcell of Land lyinge and beinge on the south side of James River in Charles Cittye Countye, Commonlye Knowne by the name of Jordans, wch. land *is now in the occupation of Captain William Rothwell.*" The Siddways, who used their property as collateral when securing their debt to the Blands, agreed not to sell any part of it until they had fully repaid what they owed. Then, on November 5, 1657, Benjamin Siddway assigned his household goods and horses to merchant John Richards, another business associate. The Siddway couple apparently defaulted on their debt to the Blands, for by January 18, 1660, "Jordans" was in their possession.

PROMOTING ECONOMIC DEVELOPMENT

Although England's Commonwealth government strengthened the Navigation Acts as a means of controlling the colony's flow of trade, Governor William Berkeley, elected to office in January 1659, quickly reminded Parliamentary officials that the colonists had the right to trade freely with "all nations in amity with the people of England." In 1660, word reached Virginia that the monarchy had been restored and that King Charles II had ascended to the throne. Governor Berkeley went to England to promote Virginia's economic interests with the newly formed Restoration government, claiming that a shortage of capital and of skilled workers kept the colony from achieving its true economic potential. But despite Berkeley's attempts to promote Virginia's economic development, Charles II paid little heed to his recommendations. Undeterred, Governor Berkeley, upon returning to Virginia, began experimenting with agricultural and industrial enterprises that showcased the colony's economic potential.

REVISING THE COLONY'S LAWS

In 1661 Virginia's legal code was revised extensively and for the first time, each county was allowed to send only two burgesses to the assembly. A year later, when the assembly formally adopted English common law, a new legal code regulated local elections, set the fees public officials could charge, and established local court procedures. Issues such as relations with the Indians, control of the quality of tobacco, and proper observance of the Sabbath also were addressed. Every county seat was to have a pillory, stocks, and whipping post near the courthouse and a ducking stool. Some of the laws enacted in 1662 were intended to strengthen Virginia's economy. Flax seed was distributed to county officials who offered it for sale. Those who raised and processed flax and wove it into cloth were eligible for a bounty. Bonuses also were offered to those who planted mulberry trees or built ships. Each county was required to have a public tan-house, where raw hides could be converted into shoe leather, and a weaver's workshop where cloth could be manufactured and made into clothing. The seat of Charles City County's court was then at Westover.

MERCHANT GEORGE POTTER OF JORDAN'S POINT

By 1660, Jordan's Point was owned by English merchant John Bland and his brother, Theodorick Bland I, whose family was highly influential in England and in Virginia. However, the property was in the hands of tenants, at least two of whom were merchants. Anthony Wyatt, who in 1652 acquired nearby Chaplin's Choice, was functioning as merchant George Potter's attorney when he paid Bland, "now proprietor," four poultry as two years' quitrent "for the land at Jordans whereon Mr. Potter dwelleth." The court record stated that Daniel Holicross, one of Potter's servants, brought the poultry to Bland at Westover, while court was in session.

George Potter, whose mercantile activities included trade with the New England colonies, probably was involved in international commerce. In January 1659, Mathew Burne or Bunn, master of George Potter's barque, the *Blackbird*, mortgaged it to William Breuton, a Rhode Island merchant. Mariner Robert Potter (perhaps a kinsman of the

Jettons, used in trade, were found at Jordan's Point at 44PG151.

Blackbird's owner) and Burne, acting as George Potter's agent, borrowed money to pay the ship's crew and to outfit the vessel with sails, rigging, cables, anchors, and provisions so that it could set sail for Virginia. But thanks to severe weather, the *Blackbird* was obliged to spend the winter in Rhode Island. Because Potter and Burne needed additional provisions and clothing for the *Blackbird's* crew, they deeded the ship to Breuton, using it as collateral. Court records dating to June 1659 reveal that William Hatcher, Henry Pryse, and Henry Randolph, all of whom lived in Henrico County, were partners in George Potter's mercantile business.

George Potter's transactions suggest that he was engaged in commerce by at least 1655 and that he was living at Jordan's Point while the property was owned by Benjamin and Mary Siddway and leased to Captain William Rothwell. In 1657 Potter was named administrator of Rothwell's estate and in 1658 he was given *quietus est* (uncontested possession) of the decedent's property. Rothwell's orphans, Robert and William, were bound to the service of George Potter until they reached age twenty-one and in exchange, he was to clothe and educate them. Concurrently, Thomas Ludson, another orphan, was bound to George Potter. Potter probably had at least one Indian servant, for in 1657 he was given permission by the local court to employ one. Daniel Holicross, who in 1660 had carried four poultry to Westover as George Potter's quitrent, also was one of his servants. In 1660 Potter released Holicross from his contract and provided him with his "freedom dues," the customary corn and clothes given to a servant who had completed his term of indenture.

SARAH POTTER OF JORDAN'S POINT

By 1663 George Potter was dead and Sarah, his widow and administrator, presented his will at court. A year later Mrs. Potter demonstrated to the justices' satisfaction that she had already expended 16,695 pounds of tobacco in settling his estate, and ultimately they concluded that she had fulfilled her legal obligations. But in 1665, when Thomas Adams' administrator won a case in the James City County court and George Potter was discovered to be one of Adams' debtors, Sarah Potter was ordered to pay 5,700 pounds of tobacco to Adams' estate, virtually all of her late husband's remaining assets. Although this transaction seemingly left Sarah Potter penniless, she may have been able to retain the 398 acres at Crabtree Neck on Flowerdew Hundred Creek that her late husband had bought from William Justice in 1662. At the time of that transaction, George Potter was described as being "of Jordans." Significantly, neither William Rothwell nor his successor, George Potter, ever actually owned the land they occupied at Jordan's Point. Instead, they leased it from the Siddways and then the Blands.

Court testimony presented in February 1666, which recounts a violent incident at Mrs. Sarah Potter's dwelling, probably took place at Jordan's Point, if her late husband's lease agreement with the Blands was still in effect. John Cogan and William Wilkins, while visiting the Potter home, became embroiled in a heated argument. Cogan allegedly seized an axe and pestle and threatened to

Image from early engraving.

dismember Wilkins. Wilkins, in turn, threw Cogan to the ground, and while the men were struggling, Mrs. Potter's dog bit Wilkins on the leg. Afterward, Cogan, who had some medical skills, treated Wilkins' leg and provided him with medicine. Sarah Potter, who witnessed the episode, gave her age as fifty when testifying in court. Mariner Robert Potter, who also was present, said that he was thirty-nine years old.

Robert Potter had been involved in the late George Potter's mercantile business during the late 1650s and may have stayed on at Jordan's and continued those operations. After the Potters vacated Jordan's Point, the Blands probably leased the tract to other tenants. In 1672 Mrs. Sarah Potter was still shipping tobacco out of Virginia.

The late 1660s would have been difficult for the Potters and anyone else living at Jordan's Point, for severe weather wrought massive destruction throughout Tidewater Virginia and the Dutch attacked the tobacco fleet. In April 1667 a violent storm that reportedly produced hail "as big as Turkey Eggs" destroyed the year's bounty of nuts, fruit and grain, "brake all the glass windowes and beat holes through the tiles of our houses," and "killed many young hogs and cattle." Then, on June 5th the Dutch sailed boldly into the mouth of the James and captured or sank twenty-some vessels heavy-laden with tobacco and awaiting the outbound tide. Mid-summer brought a rainy spell that lasted for forty days and drowned the season's crops. Finally, on August 27th, a violent hurricane struck that lasted for twenty-four hours and destroyed an estimated 10,000 houses. Heavy rain, accompanied the strong winds, caused severe flooding that forced many families from their homes. Waves lashed at the shores, causing erosion and ripping vessels from their moorings. Fallen fences released livestock that roamed about, damaging the year's tobacco and field crops.

The disasters of 1667, as a whole, must have been extremely demoralizing for the colonists. Afterward, the assembly declared August 27th a day of annual fasting and atonement, for the hurricane was attributed to "the many sins of this country" that provoked "the anger of God Almighty against us." One, perhaps both, of the storms that ripped through eastern Virginia, most likely affected those who lived at Jordan's Point.

ARCHAEOLOGICAL EVIDENCE OF THE BLANDS' TENANTS

Archaeologists from VCU studied cultural features associated with 44PG151, which is located on the east side of Jordan's Point, toward Westover. When they unearthed Structure 15, a frame dwelling with brick-floored root cellars that contained an abundance of refuse dating to the late seventeenth century, they surmised that they had found a farmstead that was occupied while the Blands owned Jordan's Point. Because a large number of mugs, jugs, table glass, and delft bowls were recovered from Structure 15, the possibility exists that it may have been the home of someone who kept a tavern or perhaps a ferry. Luxury items were relatively rare, but numerous knives, a military dagger, musket shot, and gunflints were found at the site. The presence of jettons and beads that may have been used in trade raises the possibility that 44PG151 saw use by Benjamin Siddway's renter, Captain William Rothwell; by George and Sarah Potter; or by other tenants or employees of the Blands. Near Structure 15 was a small building within a fenced yard. It may have been used to house livestock or for other agricultural purposes.

LATER USE OF JORDAN'S POINT

It is unlikely that members of the Bland family moved to Jordan's Point during the late 1660s or very early 1670s. In 1666 Sir John Pawlett conveyed Westover plantation to Theodorick Bland I who then was living at Berkeley. At Bland's death in 1671, Berkeley and Westover passed to his sons, Theodorick II and Richard, who sold Westover to William Byrd I in 1688. Because Berkeley and Westover, which had been developed as manor plantations, were available to Theodorick Bland I's sons during the 1670s and 80s, tenants probably occupied Jordan's Point. In 1670, when Augustine Herrmann prepared a map of Virginia and Maryland, indicating that buildings dotted the shore line of the colonies' navigable waterways, no structural features were then shown at Jordan's Point.

Confrontation between Governor Berkeley and the rebel Nathaniel Bacon. Courtesy of the National Park Service, Colonial National Historical Park, Jamestown Collection.

CHAPTER 7

The Blands of Jordan's Point

CATALYSTS FOR CHANGE

During the mid-1670s circumstances combined to create an administrative crisis for Governor William Berkeley, who was fractious and in failing health. Because the planter elite had solidified its power during his nearly thirty years in office, those outside the circle of privilege blamed him for most of the government's ills. Also, many people perceived political officials as opportunists who profited handsomely from performing duties that were a public trust. Personality conflicts among some of the colony's more volatile leaders added to the dissention. For example, Giles Bland of Charles City County insulted Secretary Thomas Ludwell, who promptly called for his arrest. Bland responded by calling Ludwell "a Sonne of a whore," heaped on some additional insults, and then challenged him to a duel. But it was when Bland dispatched "a mutinous and scandalous letter" to Governor William Berkeley and then forwarded a copy to England that he was thrown into jail.

Giles Bland had a good reason to be angry with Governor Berkeley and his council. Theodorick Bland I, the owner of Westover and Berkeley plantations, and his brother, English merchant John Bland, held a joint interest in Jordan's Point and some other properties. In 1671, when Theodorick Bland I died, his legal interest descended to his sons, Theodorick II and Richard. Around 1674, John Bland's son, Giles, came to Virginia to represent his father's interest in the real and personal estate that he and his late brother, Theodorick Bland I, had owned jointly. On November 18, 1674, Giles Bland initiated a law suit against his aunt, Anna Bland, widow and executrix of the late Theodorick Bland I. Then, in March 1676, Giles, as his father's legal representative, asked the General Court to partition (divide) his late uncle's estate. However, the justices decided that a debt John Bland owed to Anna Bland's father, Major General Richard Bennett, should be settled first. They also ordered Giles Bland to release several servants that he had been detaining, people who had been in Anna and Theodorick Bland

I's employ for many years. The court's decision fueled Giles Bland's animosity toward Governor Berkeley and his council, who sat as justices of the General Court.

But the colony's troubles were much more deeply rooted than squabbles among its more prominent families. Virginia planters chafed under the restraints of the Navigation Acts, which created economic problems by limiting the sale of tobacco to England. Although Governor Berkeley had urged Virginians to diversify the economy by producing manufactured goods, few people took up the cause. Colonists in the Northern Neck grew anxious when King Charles II extended its Proprietors' grant, for they worried about the legality of their land titles. Meanwhile, taxes soared. There also were troubles with the strong, warlike Indians who inhabited the interior of the continent, sometimes attacking outlying plantations and the colony's tributary natives. In addition to these concerns, there was a genuine fear of foreign invasion.

Rumors swirled through the countryside. Virginians learned of New England's Indian troubles and frontier settlers became increasingly uneasy as they waited—and waited—for their aging governor to act. Some colonists abandoned their homesteads. In March 1676 Virginia's governing officials declared war on all natives implicated in the recent attacks on frontier families. They also ordered the construction of forts at nine sites near the heads of the colony's rivers and saw that men were pressed into service to garrison them. Supplies and military equipment were procured through public levies. But many settlers grumbled about paying for the frontier forts, which they likened to expensive "mousetraps," for they realized that the blockhouses were relatively useless against roving bands of hostile Indians. They also resented Governor Berkeley's attempts to control trade with the Indians.

THE REBELLION GETS UNDERWAY

It was into this scenario that Nathaniel Bacon Jr. was thrust. The son of a wealthy English gentleman and Governor Berkeley's cousin by marriage, young Bacon was known for being quick-witted but ambitious and arrogant. He reputedly was a troublemaker whose father hastily withdrew him from Cambridge University, provided him with funds, and packed him off to Virginia. Shortly after Bacon arrived, he purchased a Henrico County plantation called Curles, in the upper reaches of the James River. In March 1675 Governor Berkeley appointed him to the Council of State, of which his uncle, Colonel Nathaniel Bacon, was a member.

Nathaniel Bacon Jr., whose plantation was attacked by Indians, agreed to lead a retaliatory march and in April 1676 set out for the southern part of the colony at the head of a band of men. Governor Berkeley, upon learning of Bacon's plans, ordered him to report to Jamestown, but Bacon demanded a commission to pursue the Indians and continued on his way. This incensed Berkeley, who declared Bacon a rebel, dismissed him from his council seat, and sent the militia after him. When Bacon reached the colony's southerly frontier, he attacked the peaceful Occoneechee (his recent allies against the Susquehannock) and seemingly made no distinction between natives, whether friend and foe. Thus began the popular uprising known as Bacon's Rebellion, which spread throughout the Tidewater region and left a bloody stain upon Virginia's history. Giles Bland embraced Nathaniel Bacon's views and, ultimately, became one of his lieutenants.

Tradition ascribes to Jordan's Point the distinction of being the site at which a group of Charles City County freeholders asked Nathaniel Bacon to lead them in an attack upon the Indians. According to a narrative prepared in 1677 by the special commissioners King Charles II sent to Virginia to investigate the causes of Bacon's Rebellion, three men, while drinking with Nathaniel Bacon at Curles, began voicing their concerns about a possible Indian assault. Because the Susquehannock Indians were known to have moved into the countryside above the falls of the James River, the men persuaded Bacon to go to the lower side of the river, to confer with that area's militiamen. Bacon and his companions reportedly took along a large quantity of rum and told the men on the south side of the river that they hoped to undertake an expedition against the Indians. The crowd became unruly and with emotions inflamed by the rum, began shouting Bacon's name and promised to support him in taking revenge upon the Indians. They also declared that if Governor Berkeley would not give him a commission, they would follow him anyhow.

Charles Andrews, an early-twentieth-century scholar, noted that one of Nathaniel Bacon's drinking companions, William Byrd I, "was a neighbor of Bacon's, sympathized with him, and as the [special commissioners'] text shows, urged him to take command of the insurgents at Jordan's Point." Andrews' confident assumption that the incident occurred at Jordan's Point has been echoed by other respected scholars, but only one piece of evidence compellingly links Bacon's Rebellion with the site called Jordan's. That solitary clue, a notation on the back of an undated petition that contextually dates to April 1676, was sent to Governor William Berkeley by a group of Charles City County citizens. They declared that the Indians had already captured and killed several local people and said that they constantly feared for their lives. They asked Governor Berkeley to grant them a commission that would allow them to defend themselves and their estates. The cover of the petition states that it was "presented to the Governor per Jordans." As the Latin word "per" can be translated as "from" or "by," the letter may have indeed originated at Jordan's Point.

Another reason the petition may be linked to Jordan's Point is that Giles Bland's father had a legal interest in the property and Giles himself was a Bacon supporter. Thus, when the Charles City County freeholders congregated on the lower side of the James River, Jordan's Point, the westernmost of the Bland-owned properties, would have been a logical rallying point.

Nathaniel Bacon returned to Curles, but set sail for Jamestown in the company of fifty armed men. Although he was seized and brought before Governor Berkeley, shortly thereafter, literally hundreds of Bacon's supporters streamed into Jamestown, determined to rescue him. With this backing, Bacon asked Berkeley's forgiveness and presented him with a written apology, which Berkeley accepted. Bacon went back to Curles, but in late June marched to Jamestown at the head of 500 men. At gunpoint, he demanded a commission to lead an expedition against the Indians and prevailed upon the burgesses to include some of his ideas in the legislation they were drafting. One of Bacon's laws authorized the seizing of Indian land, even if it meant driving the natives from their property. After the assembly adjourned, Bacon and his partisans began roving through the countryside, trying to increase their ranks and gather military stores. Bacon, perhaps to shore up his reputation as an Indian-fighter, turned his wrath toward a convenient target, the Pamunkeys, a tributary tribe that recently had signed a peace treaty with the Berkeley government. Bacon returned to Jamestown in mid-September 1676, laid siege to the town, and put it to the torch. The sight of the capital city ablaze probably made some of Nathaniel Bacon's followers wonder what would happen if Berkeley regained the upper hand.

THE REBELLION SUBSIDES

On October 26, 1676, the popular uprising was dealt a mortal blow, for Nathaniel Bacon Jr. died of the bloody flux. His successor, who lacked charisma and sense of purpose, divided the dwindling rebel army into small bands that withdrew into the countryside. Governor Berkeley's men quickly seized the opportunity to quell the insurrection and during November and December 1676 hunted down and captured many of Bacon's followers. On January 24, 1677, several of them were hauled before a military tribunal at Green Spring, where they were convicted of treason and rebellion and sentenced to death. Giles Bland was executed by Governor William Berkeley at Green Spring Plantation on March 27, 1677, at the age of twenty-nine. Bland's political connections in England, via the influence of his father-in-law, Thomas Povey, probably had created problems for Berkeley and intensified his animosity toward Bland.

In May 1677, when officials visited the dwelling of Giles Bland in Charles City County for the purpose of inventorying and confiscating his estate, his widow, Frances, informed them that "her husband came to the country with power of attorney from John Bland, in right of his father, to take [property] from the hands of Anna, the relict of Theodorick . . . and that he had no estate in Virginia of his own right." She insisted that she had no right to forfeit property that did not belong to her late husband. Frances Povey Bland's statements reveal that she and Giles were living on family-owned property, not land that belonged to them personally. As Richard Bland I was then in residence at

Berkeley, and Westover was available to his brother, Theodorick II, Giles Bland probably resided at one of the several Charles City County tracts in which his father had a legal interest.

RELATIONS WITH THE INDIANS

On May 29, 1677, a formal peace agreement was made with the colony's tributary Indians, who participated in a colorful ceremony held at Middle Plantation. The queen of the Weyanoke Indians was among the native leaders who endorsed the Treaty of Middle Plantation, kissing "the paper of peace" and affixing their signature marks. Afterward, guns were fired to commemorate the occasion and special gifts were ordered for each of the Indian leaders who had signed. By 1680 several more native leaders had signed an expanded version of the original treaty. By virtue of the Treaty of Middle Plantation, the Indians acknowledged their allegiance to the Crown and again conceded that the monarch had dominion over them and their land.

Despite the new peace agreement, sporadic outbreaks of violence continued to plague the colony's frontier, where Iroquois, Susquehannock and Seneca Indians swept down upon settlers' homesteads. Meanwhile, the tributary Indian tribes quarreled among themselves and from time to time asked the colonial government to intercede. This led some officials to declare that the recent treaty had created as many problems as it solved. In 1679 garrisons were established above the respective falls of the colony's four major rivers. In December 1682, however, the assembly voted to abolish them, for they were too costly to maintain. By 1685 the need for protection had lessened considerably, thanks to new peace agreements that involved warlike tribes beyond Virginia's borders. As troubles with the Indians often stemmed from unscrupulous trading practices, special markets were established in several places so that commerce could be controlled. The colonists employment of Indian servants (another source of ill-feeling) also commenced being regulated. In 1697, "flying armies" that consisted of a lieutenant and twelve horse soldiers were placed on constant guard above the fall line of the James, York, Rappahannock and Potomac Rivers, where they could watch over the fringes of the colony's frontiers. Tributary Indians sometimes were called upon to serve as guides.

GROWTH AND URBANIZATION

In 1680 Governor Thomas Culpeper informed the burgesses that King Charles II wanted Virginia to have towns and ports like his other colonies. The assembly responded by passing an act designed to promote urban development, trade, and manufacturing. Fifty acres of land in each of Virginia's twenty counties were to be designated official ports of entry. Bermuda Hundred was the site of Charles City County's port town. All exports after January 1, 1681, and all imports (including slaves, English servants and merchandize) after September

29, 1681, were to be sold at one of the new ports of entry. Surveyors were hired to subdivide the towns into half-acre lots whose purchasers had to improve within a year or face forfeiture. The 1680 town act offered economic incentives to would-be developers, for prices were fixed for the transportation and storage of goods in the official warehouses that were to be built in the ports. Skilled workers who set up shop in the towns were entitled to five years' immunity from prosecution for bad debt. Despite these incentives, few Virginia planters were interested in urbanization. In 1682 the king again ordered Culpeper to encourage urban development, adding that towns should be built on each of the colony's major rivers.

RESOLUTION OF THE BLAND FAMILY'S DISPUTE

In August 1678, two years after Giles Bland's execution by Governor Berkeley, John Bland of London gave his wife, Sarah, a power of attorney. He instructed her to take custody of several Virginia plantations, including Jordans, Berkeley, Kimoges, Herring Creek Mill, Westover, Upper Chippokes, Sunken Marsh plantation, Basses Choice, and a plantation at Lawnes Creek. She also was to take possession of a lot at Jamestown and all of the other land, servants, slaves, and chattels in which her husband had a legal interest. Therefore, Sarah Bland was prepared to pursue division of the family-owned real and personal estate, legal action that had been initiated by her son, Giles, in 1674. She immediately set sail for Virginia to address the tasks at hand and on February 17, 1679, had her husband's letter of authorization entered into the records of Charles City County's court.

Although little information is available about the settlement of the Bland estate, the minutes of the April 3, 1687, session of the Charles City County court state that, "Madam Sarah Bland appears and surrenders all her right to tract of land, which she, by her attorney, acknowledged to Richard Bland [son of Theodorick I] last December, the land commonly called Jordan's." Thus, up until that time, John Bland and his closest heirs shared a legal interest in the Jordan's Point tract with Theodorick Bland I's son and heir, Richard. On October 20, 1690, Richard Bland I appeared before the General Court at Jamestown, and had entered into the record Samuel Jordan's December 1620 patent which stated that the ancient planter's 450 acres would be doubled when his first dividend was seated.

A few months later, on April 28, 1691, when Richard Bland I received a patent for nearly 600 acres near Mason's Creek, not far from Chaplin's Choice, reference was made to 588 acres of land that Bland had inherited from his father. It consisted of the 388 acres at Jordan's Point that the late Theodorick Bland I and his brother had acquired from Benjamin and Mary Siddway on August 3, 1658, and 200 acres at Chaplin's Choice, purchased from Anthony Wyatt. Bland also received some residual acreage to which he was entitled under the headright system. In 1704, Richard Bland I was credited with 1,000 acres in what was then Prince George County, whereas John Bland's widow, Sarah, was listed with 1,455 acres in Surry.

RICHARD BLAND I'S PLANTATION AT JORDAN'S POINT

Richard Bland I, the son of Theodorick and Anna Bland, was born at Berkeley in 1665 and probably was the first of his kin to develop the Jordan's Point property into a family seat. He may have built a home at Jordan's Point soon after marrying Mary, the daughter of Thomas Swann of Surry County. Although the date of the couple's marriage is uncertain, it probably was around 1687, when Sarah Bland relinquished her legal interest in Jordan's Point, to her nephew, who was then twenty-two years old.

Bottle with seal bearing Richard Bland I's initials found at 44PG151. VDHR photo.

Thus, Richard Bland I probably built a dwelling there as soon as he felt confident that his land title was unencumbered. Together, Mary and Richard Bland I produced at least seven children, none of whom survived infancy. After Mary Swann Bland's death, Richard Bland I remarried. On February 1, 1701, he took as his bride, Elizabeth, the daughter of William Randolph of Turkey Island, who was twenty years his junior. Elizabeth and Richard Bland I, lived at Jordan's Point, or Jordan's, as it was known, and reared their five children: Mary, Elizabeth, Anna, Theodorick, and Richard II. Son and heir Richard Bland II was born on May 6, 1710. The Bland family's domestic complex, which has been examined by archaeologists, has been designated 44PG151.

Richard Bland I, like his father, prospered and quickly rose to prominence in political affairs. He served as a county justice and a member of the House of Burgesses, representing Charles City County and its descendant, Prince George County. As the son of Theodorick Bland I, who had been speaker of the assembly and a member of the Council of State, and as the husband of a Randolph, Richard Bland I was well connected socially and politically. Bland purchased several parcels near Jordan's Point, adding to the 1,000-acre estate that he owned in 1704. On March 5, 1714, he bought fifty acres from William Cureton, a parcel that lay directly behind the Jordan's Point acreage and in the immediate vicinity of Jenny Creek's branch, Cureton Creek. Two years later he acquired 300 acres in Westover Parish, a tract called the Great Swamp. Then, in 1718 he invested in property at the mouth of Buckskin Creek, on the Nottoway River.

Tobacco being loaded for shipment. Courtesy of the Library of Congress.

The diary kept by William Byrd II of Westover from 1709 to 1712 indicates that he and Richard Bland I were friends as well as peers. In February 1709 Bland visited Westover and gossiped about the politics of the Prince George County court. On another occasion, Bland paused at Westover while on his way home and later that evening, Byrd had his boatmen transport Bland across the river to Jordan's. Elizabeth Randolph Bland also was one of Byrd's friends and on April 11, 1711, he noted in his diary that he had visited Jordan's to express his condolences on her father's death.

Richard Bland I made his will on February 4, 1719, and died at Jordan's Point on April 10, 1720, barely having outlived his second wife, Elizabeth. Bland, who described himself as "sick and weak in body" but of sound mind, distributed his wife's personal effects along with his own. Richard Bland I bequeathed to his son, Theodorick, some land at Pigeon Swamp that he had purchased from William Randolph; some acreage at Jones Hole; and a tract on a tributary of the Nottoway River that he had bought in 1718. He left the remainder of his land, including the family's manor plantation at Jordan's, to son Richard Bland II.

Each of Richard Bland I's daughters (Elizabeth, Mary and Anna) received an identical bequest from their father: 500 pounds sterling, a feather bed and furniture, a dozen silver spoons, a horse, a woman's saddle, and two young female slaves. Bland also left the late Elizabeth Randolph Bland's wearing apparel and "other ornaments" to his daughters, noting that they were to be divided equally. The testator asked his executors to divide equally between his two sons the slaves that were not given to his daughters. The distribution was to take place as soon as Richard Bland II (who was ten years old at the time of his father's death) attained his majority.

Richard Bland I told his executors to give a mourning ring to his late wife's sister and to her brothers and their wives and children. He appointed his executors as his children's guardians and stipulated that they were not to be allowed to choose their own custodians. He instructed his executors to divide the residue of his estate between his two sons, after his just debts had been satisfied and the cost of clothing and maintaining his children had been deducted. Richard Bland I expressed his wish that "my executors not be obliged by any order of court to inventory my estate but that fair accounts be kept of the profits and loss of the same." Thus, he exercised a privilege

Top: Slaves were considered personal property that could be bought, sold, and transferred by bequest. Courtesy of The Virginia Gazette. Bottom: The Blands, like most of their peers, farmed with slave labor and provided their slaves with housing. Courtesy of the author.

accorded to those whose estates were known to be more valuable than their debts. When the late Richard Bland I's will was presented at court on April 12, 1720, no inventory was entered into the records. His son, Richard II, who was almost ten years old, was entrusted to the care of Richard and William Randolph II.

44PG151: THE BLAND FARMSTEAD

The manor house of Richard Bland I, the main dwelling at 44PG151, was located on the northeast side of Jordan's Point. It was a large earthfast house that had a brick-lined cellar or buttery. VCU archaeologists concluded that it was constructed around 1680 and was occupied until around 1730, a decade after Richard Bland I's demise. Nearby were three small earthfast outbuildings, one of which had a brick-lined basement, a garden, and a pond. A wine bottle seal found at 44PG151 is marked *R. Bland*. The main dwelling at the site, designated Structure 2, was located on a tract that an 1815 plat of Jordan's Point attributed to "Richard Bland."

When archaeologists from the JRIA studied Richard Bland I's domestic complex, they determined that the main house was a hall and parlor dwelling that was twenty feet wide and thirty-two feet long and was supported by a series of wooden posts. The remains of two of those posts, which were in a remarkably good state of preservation, were found in two postholes. Attached to the western

Jordan's Point environs as shown on Joshua Fry and Peter Jefferson's map.
Courtesy of the Library of Congress.

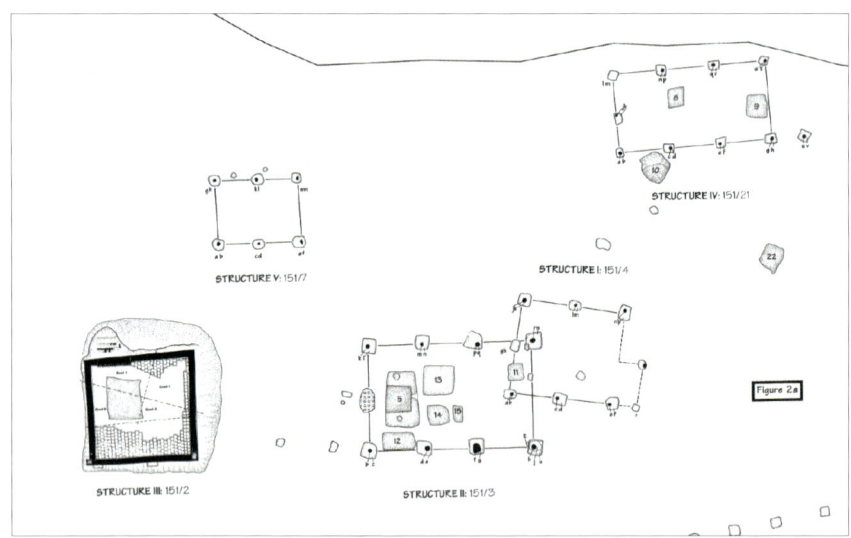

Cultural features found at 44PG151. Courtesy of James River Institute for Archaeology.

end of the dwelling was a shed or closet that measured ten-and-a-half feet by fifteen-and-a-half feet. The Blands' hall, which also was on the western end of the house, consisted of two bays. An external wood-and-clay fireplace probably served as the dwelling's heat source, as there was no evidence of a brick chimney. The parlor was twelve feet long. The Bland

The Blands were involved in an expansive trading network. Courtesy of the Mariner's Museum.

dwelling had a wooden floor and a pan tile roof, and probably had casement windows. The interior walls were plastered and archaeological evidence suggests that some of them were painted blue. Artifacts found at the site suggest that the Blands occupied a well-appointed home that reflected their superior socioeconomic status. Also present at 44PG151 were small quantities of ceramics that date somewhat later in the eighteenth century, notably creamware and Whieldon ware which date to 1740-1770. They probably reflect occupancy by subsequent generations of the Bland family or their tenants.

The several root cellars associated with the main dwelling at 44PG151 contained a mixture of artifacts that dated to the early eighteenth century but also attest to the site's use by European colonists during the early seventeenth century. One root cellar, which contained an abundance of artifacts, yielded the base of a white salt-glazed tea bowl, brass sleeve links, a William III coin weight that dates to ca. 1694-1702, an iron mortising axe, an iron wedge, an iron fireplace tong, and several tinned brass decorations for a leather harness. A bone gaming piece, fashioned in the shape of a fish, was found in this deposit and probably was used in the

Fish carved from bone, probably for the game called Loo. VDHR photo.

game called "Loo," a popular eighteenth century pastime. Fragments of bone fan blades that had been carved, pierced, and decorated in chinoiserie style also were found.

Another nearby root cellar yielded prehistoric pottery, an early-seventeenth-century pipe bowl, and two ca. 1618-1660 jettons. Among the household items unearthed were brass tacks, a brass thimble, a brass drawer pull, mirror glass, straight pins, and tableware glass. Significant quantities of delftware were found, approximately half of which were of English origin. Many were plates whose decoration reflects the popularity of designs patterned after Chinese porcelain. Delftware, stoneware, and Chinese porcelain vessels for the serving of beverages (notably punch, coffee, and tea) were present in abundance at 44PG151, reflecting some of the significant changes in foodways that occurred in colonial Virginia during the late seventeenth and early eighteenth centuries. A fragment of Rhenish stoneware, bearing the cipher of Queen Anne (1702-1714) was found as was a piece of window glass, inscribed "Mar," perhaps evidence of the presence of Richard Bland I's first wife, Mary Swann, or Richard Bland II's wife, Martha Macon Massie.

A root cellar found in the southwest corner of the hall of the Bland home contained pieces of white salt-glazed stoneware and an English tobacco pipe bowl. Also found were an iron fish hook, a brass tinker's dam, the handle of a pewter spoon, and the rim of an iron skillet. Sherds of colonoware were present, as were prehistoric materials and a fragment of a piece of armor, evidence of the site's long-term use. A second root cellar located in the floor of the Bland's hall contained a fragment of New England slipware, which suggests that it was backfilled around 1740. Among the items found in this root cellar were wine glass fragments and a piece of a Chinese porcelain coffee or chocolate cup (tangible evidence of the Blands' affluence), along with several utilitarian objects: an iron chisel, a possible gouge, an iron triangular file, and an iron plow coulter. Among the most surprising finds was an iron mud anchor. Large concentrations of plaster, which accumulated when the dwelling was destroyed, were covered by building rubble.

Structure 4, one of the dependencies associated with the Bland family dwelling, was especially elaborate and stood upon a brick foundation that was nearly twenty feet square. A bulkhead entrance at the northwest corner provided access to a brick-lined basement and a timber-lined pit. The basement's floor was brick-tiled and there was a shelved and partitioned storage area in the southwest corner. Two intact wine bottles were found upright on the tile floor, within what appears to have been a wooden storage compartment, perhaps a wine bin. The basement fill was extraordinarily rich in cultural materials. A total of thirteen *RB* wine bottle seals were recovered along with pieces of at least 158 ceramic vessels. Also found was a Westerwald stoneware chamber pot fragment and an intact wine bottle whose seal bore the initials *FP*, perhaps associated with Francis Poythress, one of Richard Bland I's in-laws. Most of the artifacts recovered from Structure 4 dated to the second quarter of the eighteenth century, although some creamware sherds were found, presumably deposited after the basement no longer was in use. Fragments of charred plaster, melted brass, and burned ceramics suggest that the building was destroyed by a devastating fire.

During the 1992-1993 field season, VCU archaeologists studied Structure 15, another building associated with 44PG151. They surmised that it was a dwelling that had been occupied by a moderately comfortable household that had an abundance of material goods but lacked luxuries. Knives, a military dagger, musket shot, and gunflints were found at Structure 15, which may have belonged to one of the Bland family's farm managers, an artisan, or perhaps a tenant.

In close association with the Bland domestic complex, and to the south of the main dwelling, was a large, fence-enclosed garden. In its northwest corner, archaeologists discovered evidence of a gate that would have provided access from the direction of the house. The garden, which was rectangular, measured 121 ½ feet long by 276 ¾ feet wide. Near the garden gate was a small building, probably a shed that had open sides. Artifacts found in association with this structure suggest that it was present at the time of the Blands' occupation. Evidence of a large pond or watering hole was found near the garden fence. The pond, which was aligned with north side of the garden, seems to have served purely utilitarian purposes. Architectural material, ceramic fragments, and prehistoric ceramics and lithics were recovered from the pond. Two human burials were found at 44PG151, one of which was a Native American and the other, European.

When Dr. Joanne Bowen and her staff at the Colonial Williamsburg Foundation analyzed the faunal remains recovered from 44PG151, they determined that by the end of the seventeenth century, the consumption of game and wild fowl declined significantly, comprising only ten percent of the total meat diet. Domestic animals had become the main source of meat and beef comprised approximately sixty-five percent of the meat consumed. This contrasts to the forty-four percent that characterized the early part of the century. Pork consumption remained steady at thirty to forty percent and mutton began to be consumed in small quantities. The Blands also enjoyed seafood and dined upon sturgeon, gar, herrings, alewife, sucker, catfish, pickerel, and white perch, utilizing far more local fish than their predecessors had.

Portrait of Richard Bland II by Susan Brown. Courtesy of Richard Bland College.

CHAPTER 8

Entering A New Era

RICHARD BLAND II

Richard Bland II, who lost his parents at age ten, lived with the Randolphs and was educated by tutors. He attended the College of William and Mary and on March 29, 1730, shortly before his nineteenth birthday, he married Ann, the seventeen-year-old daughter of Peter Poythress. At first, the young couple may have lived on the Jordan's Point plantation he had inherited. On the other hand, because of their youth, they may have resided briefly with older family members. Richard II and Ann Poythress Bland built a home at Jordan's Point and together produced twelve children: Richard III, Theodorick, Elizabeth, Edward, Ann, Sarah, Peter, Susan, John, Lucy, Mary, and William. Ann died in 1758 and a year later he married Martha Macon Massie, who lived only a short time. In June 1768, Colonel Richard Bland II's daughter, Sally (Sarah), married Robert Goode of Henrico at the Bland family home at Jordan's. Later, Colonel Bland wed Elizabeth Blair Bolling, who survived until 1775.

Richard Bland II became a prosperous planter and successful lawyer. He gradually rose in political prominence and began serving as a justice in Prince George County's monthly court. From 1742 to 1776 he represented the county in the assembly. Bland was appointed to the Committee of Correspondence and went on to become a delegate to the Virginia Conventions of 1775-1776. He was part of the delegation Virginia sent to the First Continental Congress in 1775 and was elected to serve in the Second

A tobacco seal. Courtesy of the Colonial Williamsburg Foundation, Department of Archaeological Research.

Continental Congress. In 1775-1776 he was a member of the Virginia Committee of Public Safety and was instrumental in drafting Virginia's first constitution. Bland resigned on account of ill health and returned to Virginia, where he continued serving in the House of Burgesses. He died at Mr. Tazewell's in Williamsburg on October 26, 1776, and was buried at Jordan's Point. The decedent's son and executor, Richard Bland III, placed an announcement in the *Virginia Gazette*, indicating that he intended to dispose of his late father's personal estate in Prince George County.

Richard Bland II, a man of strong opinions, believed that the legislature should be the ultimate governing body for a colony's internal affairs. He was opposed to the Church of England's establishing an American bishopric, for he believed that local vestries were better prepared to address parish needs. Some of Bland's views resulted in his being satirized by a sharp-witted writer who took him to task in the *Virginia Gazette*.

THE BLAND PLANTATION

By 1742 a tobacco inspection station had been built at Jordan's Point on the land of Richard Bland II. The facility operated in tandem with the inspectorate that was downstream at Maycock's, on Powells Creek. Whenever tobacco inspection warehouses were located on major rivers, they typically were situated at the mouths of navigable creeks. Therefore, the inspectorate at Jordan's probably was situated near the entrance to Jenny or Chappell Creeks, rather than on the river bank at a more exposed site. In 1774 the jointly-operated inspectorate was divided, an indication that each warehouse was doing enough business to become self-sustaining. A tobacco inspection warehouse continued to operate on the Blands' land at Jordan's Point until at least 1775. Historical maps prepared during the third and fourth quarters of the eighteenth century identify Jordan's Point as a topographic feature but do not depict the location of the Bland family seat, which archaeological evidence suggests was on the west side of the promontory. They also do not show the tobacco inspection facility that was somewhere on the plantation.

In late May 1771, when a devastating flood that occurred, the Bland plantation at Jordan's Point may have been affected. A news account in the May 30, 1771, edition of the *Virginia Gazette* stated that ships anchored in the James River were endangered by large trees that were swept along by an uncommonly strong current. Vessels anchored at City Point were torn from their moorings and carried downstream to Jordan's Point. At Farrar Island, Eppes Island, and other low-lying areas, the flood tide reportedly stripped away the top soil, leaving only sand and gravel and ruining the land for agriculture. The flood claimed several lives, drowned livestock, destroyed buildings, and spoiled crops. Afterward, Richard Bland II commented that "We in the lower part of the Country" had been surprised by the flood, for there was no warning of a storm. He added

The inventory of Richard Bland III's estate, compiled in 1786, included oxen. Photo by David K. Hazzard.

that "The Rivers rose to the amazing Hight [sic] of forty feet perpendicular above the common Level of the Water." Afterward, the riverbanks were covered with thick deposits of sand, animal carcasses, and debris. Bland said that much of the tobacco stored in public warehouses had been destroyed by the severe flooding and that this loss had changed merchants' perspective. A natural disaster of such proportions probably left an imprint upon Jordan's Point and the Bland plantation seat, which overlooked the river. The impact of raging flood waters, racing toward the Chesapeake Bay, would have been particularly strong on the west or upstream side of Jordan's Point, where archaeologists believe that Richard Bland II's home was located.

44PG303

Archaeological excavations undertaken at 44PG303 by Dr. William M. Kelso and Monticello archaeological field school students in 1987 tentatively identified 44PG303 as the eighteenth-century house occupied by Richard Bland II. An opportunity for a more thorough examination by VCU archaeologists in 1992 resulted in a somewhat different conclusion. They proffered that the building designated 44PG303 was built between 1760 and 1770 and was destroyed within a relatively short time. They also noted that construction (or perhaps elaboration) of the domestic complex may have come to a halt in 1776 when Richard Bland II died or when the American Revolution got underway. The house was located on the west side of Jordan's Point, near its tip. Assuming that the original Bland home, 44PG151, was abandoned around 1730 and that construction at 44PG303 got

Chimney base found at 44PG303 and excavated by VCU archaeologists. VDHR photo.

underway around 1760, the Blands probably occupied another part of Richard II's Jordan's Point property during that interval or lived elsewhere.

The main part of the building at 44PG303 measured sixty feet long by twenty-two feet wide and had a T-shaped wing of comparable width that was thirty feet in length, perhaps reflecting a Georgian sense of proportion. External end chimneys flanked the gables of the main body of the house and another chimney may have stood at the gable end of the wing. A cross wall in the dwelling's central block suggests that it had a central passage that was flanked by two almost-square rooms. The wing addition seems to have contained two rooms. The existence of a purposefully prepared clay floor and a substantial amount of domestic debris suggests that the dwelling had an English basement that extended three feet below grade and four or five feet above grade.

The house, which stood on a rise overlooking the James River, probably was fabricated of brick or had brick end walls. Its intact footings were only one-and-a-half bricks wide, which suggests that the building was one or one-and-a-half stories in height or of frame construction. The scarcity of domestic artifacts and the absence of architectural features (such as porches, sidewalks, drains, and ancillary buildings) and landscape features (such as gardens and planting beds) together suggest that the main building at 44PG303 was destroyed soon after its construction, if indeed it was completed. The structure may well have been threatened during the 1771 flood when the James River rose to an unprecedented level and thick layers of debris were deposited along its shores.

THE DEMISE OF RICHARD BLAND II

Richard Bland II was buried at Jordan's Point in 1776, having outlived all three of his wives. Neither his will nor an inventory of his estate seemingly has survived, probably because they were recorded in the General Court, whose early records have been destroyed. However, an advertisement placed in the *Virginia Gazette* in January 1777 by the decedent's son and administrator, Richard Bland III, sheds some light upon his material possessions, which were being offered for sale at Jordan's Point. Because all of Richard Bland II's personal estate reportedly was being liquidated, his buildings at Jordan's probably were emptied of their contents. Offered for sale were thirty "very fine" slaves, "all kinds of household and kitchen furniture," a "library of books," a new chariot, a riding chair, foodstuffs (such as tea, coffee, and double-refined sugar), and utilitarian items such as smith's tools, wool and cotton cards, heckles, leather and rawhide, and a parcel of mahogany. Agricultural items included a cutting box and scythes, plus cotton and flax seed. The livestock being sold included large herds of sheep and cattle as well as hogs, horses, mares, and colts. It was likely when Richard Bland III sold his late father's personal property that Thomas Jefferson purchased items from his library, including numerous transcriptions of early Virginia records that later were re-transcribed and published in William Waller Hening's *Statutes At Large*. Some of Richard Bland II's personal correspondence survived and was published by Charles Campbell. Among those with whom Bland exchanged letters were notables such as George Washington and Patrick Henry.

THE AMERICAN REVOLUTION IN TIDEWATER VIRGINIA

By late summer 1775 the breach between Great Britain and her American colonies had become irreparable. On November 10, 1775, the *Virginia Gazette* published King George III's August 23rd declaration that the colonies were in "open and avowed rebellion" and his call-to-arms to suppress what he called an insurrection. During this period, Lord Dunmore's men, despite the Virginians' resistance, were relatively free to cruise Tidewater's navigable waterways and come ashore at will. Dunmore declared martial law in Virginia and signed an Emancipation Proclamation, freeing all slaves and indentured servants and inviting them to bear arms on behalf of the king. In May 1776, when British General Henry Clinton invaded North Carolina, Virginia troops were sent to oppose him. On June 12, 1779, the General Assembly voted to move Virginia's capital from Williamsburg to Richmond, a centralized location presumed safe from enemy attack. On April 7, 1780, the state's executive department ceased transacting business in Williamsburg and on the 24th resumed its duties in Richmond. During the first week of May, the assembly held its first session in its new capital city.

On June 12, 1779, the General Assembly voted to move Virginia's capital from Williamsburg to Richmond. Courtesy of David K. Hazzard.

In mid-April 1781 British General William Phillips arrived in Hampton Roads with an army 2,600 strong. Phillips' men marched to the mouth of the Chickahominy and boarded naval vessels that transported them to the mouth of the Appomattox River.

In late May Charles Lord Cornwallis and his army of seasoned veterans arrived in Petersburg, where they joined forces with Phillips' men, temporarily under the command of General Benedict Arnold. This union of forces created a British Army of 7,000 men. Cornwallis crossed to the upper side of the James River and set out in pursuit of the Marquis de Lafayette, who had retreated toward Fredericksburg while awaiting reinforcements. However, on June 30, 1781, Cornwallis notified his superiors that he was moving his men to the lower side of the James.

In September 1781 French troops streamed into the area, part of the overall military build-up that preceded the siege of Yorktown. By September 28th the Allied Armies were on their way to Yorktown to commence their attack. Two days later the British surrendered their outermost earthworks, where the offensive had begun, and by October 17th Cornwallis had asked the Allies to parley. The moment of victory came on October 19, 1781, when Cornwallis surrendered to the Allies and the American colonies' independence was won.

According to oral tradition, the Bland family's ancestral manor house was destroyed in 1781 when Benedict Arnold's men moved up the James River toward Richmond. Although British forces were indeed mobilized throughout the area, neither documentary nor archaeological evidence has come to light suggesting that buildings at Jordan's Point were singled out for destruction. A map prepared by a French cartographer in 1781 shows the inland route that the British took and identifies Jordan's Point by name, but it omits any structures that may have been present. Narratives written by participants in the American Revolution, most of which are detailed, make no mention of an attack, nor did Bland family members file postwar reimbursement claims for damage to their property. It is possible, however, that British naval vessels sailing past Jordan's Point found the unoccupied Bland mansion an irresistible target.

A NEW NATION TAKES ROOT

After the French and British went home, the inhabitants of eastern Virginia tried to rebuild their lives. Financial problems plagued many households during the postwar period, even though taxes were payable in agricultural commodities such as wheat, rye, oats, barley, corn, and bacon. Some prominent Virginians, who had gone heavily into debt in support of the war effort, afterward suffered the consequences. The relocation of Virginia's capital from Williamsburg to Richmond accelerated the Tidewater region's decline, for the Piedmont gained new political influence. Petersburg and Hopewell grew in size, but there was relatively little interest in urbanization on the south side of the James, except near the seacoast.

Throughout eastern Virginia, farm size was reduced as large estates were broken up and redistributed among numerous heirs. Because Virginia farmers traditionally devoted little attention to improving and maintaining their soil, long-term neglect culminated in lessened productivity. The lack of an opportunity to acquire good, arable farmland, coupled with dramatic fluctuations in agricultural prices, led to a general out-migration of eastern Virginia's white population. The opening up of western lands and the construction of internal improvements such as canals, turnpikes, and railroads fueled this trend.

DEFINING STATE GOVERNMENT

In June 1776, when the Virginia Convention adopted a constitution for the new Commonwealth of Virginia, the structure of county government stayed intact, as did the link between church and state. As a result, county courts and parish vestries, which were appointive bodies, retained their taxing authority. Many people felt that this was equivalent to taxation without representation. Theodorick Bland and Edmund Ruffin represented Prince George County in the State Convention of 1788. As time went on, some important changes proved necessary in the upper levels of government. The House of Burgesses readily evolved into the House of Delegates, but a number of new public offices (positions formerly occupied by royal appointees) had to be filled and the judicial system had to be modified. The fledgling state government had to address needs that ranged from civil defense, trade, and the monetary system, to public welfare, a responsibility formerly relegated to the Established Church.

Perhaps one of the most remarkable actions taken by Virginia's General Assembly at the close of the American Revolution was passage of legislation that permitted owners to free their slaves. The new law allowed them to bequeath slaves their freedom and they could file a deed of manumission with the county

Tobacco was sent to Richmond for processing. Courtesy of the Crown Publishing Company.

court. A substantial number of Virginians availed themselves of this opportunity and an estimated 10,000 blacks were freed during the decade. Soon, however, Virginia's tobacco-growers began lobbying for restrictions on manumission and some slaveholders argued that free blacks caused discontent among the enslaved. This backlash led to passage of a law that required freed slaves to leave the state or face re-enslavement. Famed agricultural reformer Edmund Ruffin, who inherited a riverfront plantation in Prince George County not far from Jordan's Point, was an ardent supporter of slavery.

MILITARY DEFENSE AND PROTECTION

After the close of the Revolutionary War, many Americans feared that the British would return to attack their break-away colonies. Local militia units drilled regularly in their home communities and chose their own officers, whose names were submitted to the county court. It was the governor, however, who actually commissioned military officers, a practice that was a holdover from the colonial era. Most of the men appointed to high ranks in the military served as county justices or held other relatively important government positions. Thus, even after the Revolution, prominent families like the Blands, who traditionally monopolized political power, continued to be highly influential.

In July 1796, a ship from Norfolk, whose crew had smallpox, reportedly was anchored at Jordan's Point. In early 1800 Charles Simpson recommended to the governor that a hospital be established at Jordan's Point for the reception and cure of infectious diseases. A shipboard medical facility was in operation there on August 22, 1800, when Thomas Wilcox was appointed its supervisor and the hospital's records were sent to the governor. In September 1800 George Nicolson informed the governor that it was impossible to get a doctor aboard the vessels in the quarantine ground at Jordan's Point. He said that provisions and fresh water were difficult to obtain and recommended that patients and personnel be transferred to the quarantine station at Richmond.

RICHARD BLAND III

Richard Bland III, who inherited his father's Jordan's Point plantation in 1776, may have temporarily moved into the old family home if it was habitable. However, he and his wife, Mary, the daughter of Colonel John Bolling, built a new domestic complex at a location that was much further inland but on the west side of Jordan's Point. Together, the Bland couple produced four children: Richard IV, Ann P., John B., and Eliza B.

Prince George County personal property tax rolls for 1783 credited Richard Bland III with twenty-two black slaves of tithable age, twenty-one younger slaves, twenty horses, forty-five cattle, and four wheeled vehicles. Although the quantity of taxable personal property attributed to him fluctuated slightly from year to year, it is evident that he was a wealthy and successful planter.

Richard Bland III died prior to March 30, 1786, and afterward an inventory was made of his personal effects. Nearly a year later, his real and personal property was divided among his heirs in accordance with his will, a document that seemingly has been lost or destroyed. Richard Bland III's inventory reveals that he and his family lived luxuriously on a well equipped and relatively self-sufficient plantation whose workforce included forty-seven slaves. The large quantity of black walnut furniture that was attributed to Bland's estate included a combination desk and bookcase, a corner cupboard, a desk, a press, five tables of various sizes, a chest, a tea board, and a dozen chairs. Also on hand were a dozen birch chairs and some mirrors.

The Blands' refinement and social standing is reflected by some of the other items that were in their possession. For example, in the family home were twenty-eight Queensware plates and dishes; twenty-six pewter plates and dishes; two dozen knives, forks and spoons; and specialized serving vessels such as china bowls, decanters, wine glasses, and pots for tea, coffee, and chocolate. The family was abundantly supplied with culinary equipment that would have been used in meal preparation, plus 120 pounds of coffee and nine loaves of sugar. The presence of books and a spy glass or telescope reflect family members' interest in the outside world. Richard Bland III's inventory included equipment for farming and for household tasks such as spinning, plus parcels of blacksmith's, carpenter's and shoemaker's tools and a seine for fishing. The Blands had large herds of cattle, oxen, swine, and sheep and the 150 bushels of corn and 300 bushels of wheat that were on hand probably were produced on the Jordan's Point plantation.

In October 1786, the justices of Prince George County appointed special commissioners to divide and distribute the personal estate of the late Richard Bland III. His widow, Mary, received all of his household and kitchen furniture, his chariot, four horses, twelve slaves, half of the livestock on the plantation, and half of the agricultural and utilitarian equipment.

The court-appointed commissioners assigned each of the late Richard Bland III's three surviving children equal shares of his personal estate. Richard Bland IV received four horses and ten slaves, one of whom was a boy named John Wilson, who had been devised specifically to him. Richard IV was assigned some agricultural equipment, a parcel of smith's tools, and forty-five fathoms of new line, presumably for a sailing vessel. He also inherited some livestock and a share of the corn and wheat crops. One of the late Richard Bland III's daughters, Ann Poythress Morison, received a dozen slaves, two horses, some money and livestock, and a share of the plantation's corn and wheat crops. Her sister, Elizabeth, was given a comparable number of slaves and horses, some money and livestock, and a share of the crops.

Although Richard Bland III's personal property was divided among his heirs, his landholdings were kept intact for the next several years and attributed to his estate, probably because his widow, Mary, had life-rights in the plantation. She probably continued to live in the home she and her late husband had shared and for a few years enjoyed the use (if not outright ownership) of the personal property credited to his estate. However, son Richard Bland IV married Susannah Poythress when in his teens and seems to have brought his bride to the Jordan's Point plantation he stood to inherit.

RICHARD BLAND IV OF JORDAN'S POINT

In 1787 Richard Bland IV paid county taxes upon himself and a young white male between the ages of sixteen and twenty-one named Michael Singleton, who probably was the farm manager at Jordan's Point. Bland also paid taxes on thirty-one slaves, a large herd of livestock, four vehicles, and a stud horse. The amount of taxable personal property attributed to his mother dropped sharply. By 1789, Michael Singleton was gone and Richard Bland IV had begun paying personal property tax on two young men, Thomas Singleton and Tony or Terry Wells. They were quickly replaced by Jiles (or Jessie) and Joseph Wells, who were over the age of twenty-one and perhaps were more experienced agronomists than their predecessors. In 1793, Mary Bolling Bland paid personal property tax on behalf of an overseer who was over sixteen but under twenty-one, the only year she had one in her employ. She probably died around 1802, for her name disappeared from the tax rolls. In 1798 Richard Bland IV was credited with his late father's 1,200 acre plantation, property that was attributed to him through 1805.

Richard Bland IV died on March 25, 1806, leaving a widow and several underage children. Shortly thereafter, the widowed Susannah Poythress Bland received 450 acres of the home tract, her dower third, but she probably had the right to occupy the family home. Throughout the next several years, Richard Bland IV's estate was credited with 750 acres and Susannah P. Bland, with 450 acres. When Richard Bland IV died, he had twenty-five slaves who were age sixteen or older, ten horses and a coach. By 1810 the bulk of his personal assets had been transferred to his widow, to whom they were attributed until 1820.

THE WAR OF 1812

During Thomas Jefferson's second term as president, hostilities between Great Britain and France spilled over to the United States. Shortly after war broke out, Governor James Barbour concluded that a fort should be built at Jamestown or upstream at Hood's, across from Weyanoke. However, no action was taken to secure either position. Months later, when the British invaded Virginia waters and blockaded Hampton Roads, a sense of uneasiness settled over the Tidewater region. In early February 1813 local infantrymen were sent to Norfolk and Hampton to repel a potential invasion, in essence leaving the rest of the region defenseless.

By spring 1813 the British invaders had become much more aggressive. Nicholas Faulcon of Surry County informed his brother-in-law that "Most people upon the river, above and below us, have been moving off their property for several days and some families have quitted their homes." He said that he expected the British to send plundering parties ashore whenever they needed fresh provisions. The threat the British posed was a persistent one and in late June 1813 they returned in a convoy that included two brigs, five or six schooners, and eight barges. Raiding parties went ashore, armed with swords and pistols, seizing livestock, barnyard poultry, and any other

During 1813 British naval vessels penetrated the upper reaches of the James River and seamen sometimes went ashore, wreaking destruction. Courtesy of The Virginia War Museum.

food stores they could find. On July 1, 1813, the British raided a number of homes along the south side of the James River, carrying off whatever they could and laying waste to what remained. One British officer who came ashore with a flag of truce said that his men were not supposed to be plundering.

Throughout the summer of 1813, fourteen British barges, an armed brig, and six or seven tenders moved freely up and down the James River, plundering homes near the shore and sometimes venturing inland. Tidewater residents continued to remain uneasy about the possibility of an enemy invasion, but the British failed to return. In April 1814 government officials again considered the efficacy of building a fort and battery on Jamestown Island or further upstream at Hood's. Although people on the Southside continued to be uneasy, the Treaty of Ghent, signed on Christmas Eve 1814, officially ended the war.

After hostilities ceased, Virginia entered a period of economic stagnation and America experienced its first great depression, the Panic of 1819. Agricultural prices plummeted, land prices dropped, and many Tidewater families moved west. Only when farmers learned that lime and marl would restore the fertility of soil acidified by the long-term production of tobacco, did local economic conditions begin to improve.

THE BLAND HOME

In 1815 the widowed Susannah Poythress Bland was credited with twenty slaves who were age sixteen or older and six who were between nine and sixteen. She also had eight horses, asses, or mules and thirty-four cattle and paid taxes on some household furnishings that were considered luxury items. They included several pieces of mahogany furniture, notably, a chest of drawers with a desk, two dining tables, a tea table, and a dozen "common" chairs that were ornamented. She also had another chest of drawers with a desk that was considered taxable. Richard Bland V, who was in his early twenties and probably was living in the family home, paid taxes on himself and a horse.

In 1815 the late Richard Bland IV's Jordan's Point plantation was surveyed and subdivided so that it could be distributed equitably among his living children. According to the surveyor's notes, the decedent's property at Jordan's, "where he resided," included a total of 1,754 acres. Sally Bland Batt, a married daughter, received seventeen acres at the tip of Jordan's Point, called the Jordan's Point Fishery, plus 500 acres known as the Beaver Castle. Theodorick Bland was allotted 230 acres that spanned the point and lay inland, directly behind the Fishery. His parcel included the family graveyard. Richard Bland V received 230 acres that were located south of the tract assigned to his brother, Theodorick, and encompassed part of the road that ran to the Fishery. John B. Bland, who was fifteen years old, was assigned a 150 acre tract that contained a house and dependency and was adjacent to Richard V's parcel. Mary Bland was given 300 acres that straddled Cureton Swamp and abutted Bikars (now Chappell) Creek.

Peter Bland, whose property lay furthest inland and away from the waterfront, received 392 acres.

The dwelling and dependency shown on the plat that was made in 1815, when the Bland plantation was subdivided, probably was the family home erected during the lifetime of Richard Bland IV, for when he died in 1806, all of his living children were minors. Historical maps and tax records suggest that the Bland domestic complex stood until the close of the Civil War. It was oriented toward overland transportation corridors, which would have connected the Blands with urban markets in Petersburg and Hopewell. This shift away from the James River may reflect a change in the Blands' usage of their land.

In 1815 the late Richard Bland IV's Jordan's Point plantation was subdivided and apportioned among his heirs. Prince George County Surveyors Record Book 1 (1794-1825), p. 244.

Although the Jordan's Point plantation was surveyed and partitioned in 1815, the late Richard Bland IV's property was not distributed among his heirs until five years later. The bulk of his acreage continued to be credited to his estate and the widowed Susannah Bland's landholdings remained constant. In 1820, when Virginia's tax commissioners began listing the total value of the buildings on the properties they assessed, improvements worth $1,000 were attributed to Richard Bland IV's estate, then described as 889 ¾ acres on the James River. Land records reveal that those buildings stood upon the acreage that in 1815 was assigned to the decedent's son, John B. Bland. Meanwhile, Susannah Bland had only 232 acres, property that was undeveloped. As time went on, the late Richard Bland IV's real estate was distributed among his heirs. Census records reveal that in 1820 Susannah Poythress Bland's household included five white males and three white females who were between sixteen and twenty-six. Also present was a man who was between twenty-six and forty-five and a woman who was age forty-five or older, probably Susannah. Enslaved household members included twelve men and boys and seventeen women and girls, but six slaves were age forty-five or older. A total of fourteen people in Mrs. Bland's household were involved in agriculture. In 1826, the late Richard Bland IV's land was described as 251 acres on the James River that had buildings worth $1,000.

In 1826 Theodorick Bland's name commenced appearing in the tax rolls but he had no taxable personal property, perhaps because he was only twenty-one and still living at home. Then, in 1830, John B. Bland's name was listed. Census records indicate that in 1830 Susannah Poythress Bland headed a large household that included a white man between twenty and thirty (Theodorick) and another who was between thirty and forty. Also present was a white woman who was between fifteen and twenty and another who was between sixty and seventy, plus three girls who were under the age of fifteen. Mrs. Bland's household included forty-three people, most of whom were enslaved. Among them were four men and two women who were between the ages of fifty-five and one hundred. John B. Bland was then living elsewhere in Prince George County, in a separate household that included an elderly white woman and some slaves. Susannah Poythress Bland transferred her taxable personal property to her son, Dr. Theodorick Bland, a physician, in 1833, and a year later he married Mary B. Harrison of Brunswick County.

Tax records reveal that during the early 1830s, Susannah and her son, Dr. Theodorick Bland, swapped parcels of land. She began accumulating real estate, in time acquiring the home tract that in 1815 had been allocated to John B. Bland. However, by 1839 the structures on that property were gone. In 1840, Dr. Bland acquired Susannah's acreage and had in all, 981 acres that were devoid of buildings. During this period he may have been purchasing his siblings' acreage in an attempt to reconstitute the family's holdings.

In 1843, Dr. Theodorick Bland was credited with the unimproved land that he had had three years earlier, plus 190 acres that contained $421 worth of buildings. He also had three tracts of land on Wards Creek that he had inherited from William I. Bishop. Dr. Bland had around twenty slaves, a dozen horses, and a gold watch, an item physicians often possessed.

In 1840 Dr. Theodorick Bland headed a household that included thirty-one people, eleven of whom were involved in agriculture. He was between thirty and forty years old and his wife was between twenty and thirty. The Blands had three children under the age of five and the family included twenty-two slaves, more than half of whom were of prime working age. A decade later, census records indicated that Dr. Bland was a forty-five-year-old farmer and his wife, Mary, was age forty. Then living in the family home were the couple's three young children and twenty-year-old Ann P. Bland, Dr. Bland's sister.

TIDEWATER VIRGINIA'S AGRICULTURAL ECONOMY AT MID-CENTURY

During the mid-nineteenth century, improved agricultural techniques and reduction in farm size led to a revitalization of the region's economy. The cultivation of tobacco, which for generations played a vital role in Tidewater farming, was replaced by the production of grain crops. By the time of the Civil War, the region's agriculture had evolved into a mixed crop system. Grains predominated, especially wheat and corn, followed in importance by potatoes. Cattle production for beef and dairy products and other forms of animal husbandry also were on the ascent. Agricultural diversification offset over-dependency upon a single crop's success.

Agricultural census records, first tabulated in 1850, shed light upon the scope of Dr. Theodorick Bland's farming operations. He was credited with 500 acres that were improved and 600 acres that were not; the cash value of his farm was $30,000. Dr. Bland owned $300 worth of farming implements and a large and valuable herd of livestock that included horses, asses, mules, cattle (including oxen and dairy cows), and swine. Butter was made at Jordan's Point and perhaps sold. Dr. Bland's farmland produced more than twice as much corn as it had wheat, plus some peas, beans, and Irish potatoes. The productivity of the Bland farm suggests that the physician was an enlightened farmer who availed himself of the latest advances in agricultural technology.

In 1851, Dr. Theodorick Bland's Jordan's Point property, which had been vacant since 1839, had newly constructed buildings worth $1,825. He also had disposed of his other acreage, perhaps to raise the funds he needed to develop his home farm.

According to oral tradition, members of the Bland family called Dr. Theodorick Bland's new home at Jordan's Point the "shed house." Dr. Bland's son, Theodorick ("Uncle Thee") described the dwelling as one-and-a-half stories high, T-shaped, and set back from the river. The house, which was situated on a hill, was surrounded by dependencies that included granaries, storehouses, a large carriage house, a stable, and slave cabins. To the east was a large spring. Tax records indicate that Dr. Theodorick Bland's home stood until the close of the Civil War. Maps prepared by military cartographers suggest that Dr. Bland's residence was the only house in the vicinity of Jordan's Point and that it stood on or near the site previously occupied by the dwelling of his father, Richard Bland IV.

In 1855, the tax assessor credited Dr. Theodorick Bland with twenty-five slaves over the age of twelve and a large herd of livestock that included horses, cattle, sheep, and swine. His taxable personal possessions included $200 worth of household and kitchen furniture, some gold and silver jewelry, and a carriage. The assessor noted that Dr. Bland had sold one-and-one-half acres of his land at Jordan's Point to the United States government. Historical maps indicate that a lighthouse was built at the tip of Jordan's Point on what in 1815 had been the Fishery tract. The first lighthouse consisted of a keeper's quarters that had a red pressed-glass light on its roof.

In 1857 Prince George County's tax assessor consolidated Dr. Theodorick Bland's tracts of land, describing the unified parcel as 1,071-and-one-half acres called "Jordans Point" that had $1,825 worth of buildings. In 1858, when the assessor began making note of where landowners were residing, he indicated that Dr. Theodorick Bland was then living on his Jordan's Point property.

Dr. Theodorick Bland died during the winter of 1859, and in 1860 the assessor noted that his home tract was in the possession of his widow, Mary B. Bland, under the terms of the physician's will. The property was listed in her name until 1863, at which time it was credited to her estate. In 1860 Mary B. Bland paid personal property taxes on twenty-five slaves who were age twelve or older and she had horses, cattle, sheep, swine, and a pleasure carriage. Census records for 1860 indicate that Mary, who was age fifty, owned $32,000 worth of real estate and $54,000 worth of personal property. She shared the family home with her daughters, who ranged in age from eight to fourteen, and her thirteen-year-old son. Farm manager William Clements, who was age twenty-six, lived with the Blands, as did a woman identified as S. H. Cargill, who was age thirty-four and may have been a housekeeper.

The Harrison Bridge. Photo by David K. Hazzard

CHAPTER 9

The Beginning of the End

NORTH AGAINST SOUTH

The first shots fired at Fort Sumter, South Carolina, on April 12, 1861, signaled the beginning of the Civil War. Although politicians North and South had heatedly debated secession, neither side seems to have realized that the issues under dispute would culminate in a long, bloody war. When President Abraham Lincoln issued a call to arms, the response was enthusiastic. Several states in the upper South quickly aligned themselves with the Confederacy. On April 17, 1861, Virginia joined the Confederacy, and on May 23rd the state's voters ratified a secession ordinance. At that juncture, the Confederacy's seat of government was moved from Montgomery, Alabama, to Richmond, Virginia. From then on, the focus of the war in the east was on the territory separating Richmond from Washington, D. C., the federal capital.

Shortly after Virginia passed the Ordinance of Secession, General Robert E. Lee was named military advisor to President Jefferson Davis and the Armies of the Potomac, the Valley, the Rappahannock, the Peninsula and Norfolk were put into the field. In late summer 1861, the Confederate Army's forces in Virginia were concentrated in the northern part of the state, which left the peninsula open to an advance, especially from the direction of Fort Monroe, the Union Army's stronghold.

Defending the homeland. Photo by David K. Hazzard.

In spring 1862, General Lee was responsible for seeing that Richmond was well defended. His ability to do so proved far more important than anyone could have predicted, for by the end of the war, a total of seven military campaigns had been launched

An advance of the cavalry skirmish line by Edwin Forbes. Courtesy of the Library of Congress.

against the Confederate capital. Lee fortified sites along the James River, hoping to control water access to Richmond. He had earthworks built at old Fort Powhatan, Hardins Bluff, and other locations. Collectively, these gun emplacements were intended to prevent Union naval vessels from circumventing any land-based defenses the Confederates built on the peninsula.

WAR IN THE LOWER TIDEWATER REGION

Early in 1862, Union military leaders undertook a drive to capture Richmond and bring the war to a timely end. The offensive became known as the Peninsula Campaign. Thanks to the considerable tactical skill of John B. Magruder, the Union Army's advance was delayed long enough for the Confederate Army to slip away to the outskirts of Richmond.

Although skirmishes occurred at Cabin Point and City Point in 1862, it was on May 5, 1864, that Union General B. F. Butler landed 30,000 men at City Point and Bermuda Hundred, at the mouth of the Appomattox River, intending to move against Richmond via Petersburg. Between May 5th and May 11th, Union cavalry undertook raids in the vicinity of Petersburg and later in the month fighting occurred at City Point, which ultimately became a staging area and supply point. On October 16, 1864, Union troops from City Point ventured into Prince George and Surry Counties on a reconnaissance mission. Troop movements often occurred along the Jordan's Point Road. In late March 1865 President Abraham Lincoln took his wife and son to City Point, intending to combine a family vacation and a conference with General Ulysses S. Grant. Lincoln and

Grant conferred on March 25th. Then, the president took the military railroad to Petersburg, mounted up, and on horseback toured the lines around the city. On March 27th and 28th Lincoln met with Generals Grant and Sherman and Admiral Porter aboard the vessel *River Queen*, which was anchored at City Point. He stayed on through April 1st so that he could keep abreast of Grant's progress. The Confederates retained Petersburg

Jordan's Point and vicinity as depicted on S. L. Sommers' "Map of Prince George County, Virginia, 1864." Courtesy of the Library of Virginia.

even though Union troops were entrenched at City Point and Bermuda Hundred. It was during the Civil War that many of Prince George and Charles City counties' court records were destroyed.

Maps made during the Civil War identify Jordan's Point, the so-called "Indian Field Point" at the mouth of Jenny Creek, and the Bland home. The residence stood at a location analogous to the one at which a dwelling stood in 1815, when the family's property was partitioned. One cartographer identified by name the Beaver Castle Fishery and indicated that six buildings then stood within the boundaries of the Bland tract as it was defined in 1815. Other mapmakers' works confirm this interpretation.

SURRENDER AT APPOMATTOX

On April 9, 1865, General Robert E. Lee decided to meet with General Ulysses S. Grant to negotiate the terms of surrender. The two military leaders conferred in the McLean house at Appomattox and drafted a document they signed at 4 P.M. The Confederates, weary, half-starved, and disheartened, marched through lines of Union infantry and laid down their arms, while Union troops watched or stood guard. Lee's surrender heralded the end of the war, but at that juncture, one form of suffering yielded to another.

THE AFTERMATH OF WAR

For the first six months after the surrender at Appomattox, at least 25,000 white Virginians subsisted on army rations, as did many of the 360,000 newly freed blacks who lacked food, clothing, shelter, and the means to make a living. The 13th Amendment to the U. S. Constitution was ratified, ending slavery and the old social order to which much of the South had been accustomed. Real estate values plummeted and land worth $50 an acre before the war afterward sold for $2. So massive was the damage to Virginia's industrial establishment that it was the only state failing to attain its prewar production levels by 1870. In sum, the war, followed by military occupation and Reconstruction, exacted so great a toll that Virginia was reduced to poverty and despair.

Undoubtedly, many returning soldiers, already weary, malnourished and saddened by the loss of comrades, were completely demoralized by the conditions they found at home, for they were confronted with what must have seemed like an insurmountable array of problems. Recovery took time, money, ingenuity and a tremendous amount of hard work.

Local court records reflect the hardships of Reconstruction, some of which lingered for a decade or more. Some people, thanks to the loss of farm income, were unable to finish paying for property they had begun purchasing before the war. Others became indebted to merchants and various business establishments. Labor shortages, worn out agricultural equipment, and farmland overgrown with brambles, weeds, and small trees that defied the plow, were among the numerous problems farmers faced. They also lacked the funds they needed to buy seed, fertilizer, and livestock. As a result, many people fell deeply into debt due to circumstances that were beyond their control. Ultimately, a significant number were obliged to forfeit their real and personal property or declare bankruptcy. The state's economy was crippled by indebtedness that lingered for several years. The destruction of many of Prince George County's antebellum court records would have made it difficult for those buying or selling land to substantiate ownership claims.

After the war, many African Americans struggled to survive. Harper's Weekly, May 21, 1870.

In time, immense changes occurred in Virginia's agricultural economy. Right after the war, many of Tidewater's farm families shifted to less labor-intensive forms of agriculture, such as animal husbandry, or raising fruit and vegetable crops that could be sold in urban markets. Some farms were operated by leaseholders or sharecroppers, such as landless African-Americans, who had few options and sometimes chose to remain in their former neighborhoods. Virginia's agricultural productivity dropped by more than half and many rural landowners were forced to subdivide their farms or relinquish them altogether. Northern speculators with expendable capital sometimes seized the opportunity to purchase cheap land, often for back taxes, and quickly resold or subdivided it, hoping to turn a quick profit.

POST-WAR CONDITIONS AT JORDAN'S POINT

In 1865 the assessor noted that the structural improvements on Mary B. Bland's farm, Jordan's Point, were gone and in 1866, he wrote "$1,825 deducted for destruction of buildings." They may have fallen prey to the Union Navy's gunboats that frequently plied the James River, sometimes firing at the buildings they passed. Dr. Theodorick Bland's son, Theodorick or "Uncle Thee," a Confederate Army veteran, said that when it came his turn to take charge of the home place, "there was nothing left but the ground." He also stated that whenever "the Union Army was camped around," the soldiers "nearly obliterated everything." In another piece of correspondence, Bland said that the "shed house" had been let to renters until the Union Army occupied the place during 1864 and 1865, "leaving everything in a dilapidated condition." He added that the "old building was damaged very much" and that only the kitchen and a store room survived. He added that the home place was let to tenants after the war. But if the assessor's records are accurate, by 1866 the tract was devoid of buildings or they were in such poor condition that they were deemed untaxable. In the 1870s, the remains of the old house and kitchen reportedly burned.

In 1869 the real estate owned by the late Dr. Theodorick Bland and his wife, Mary B., was partitioned and court-appointed commissioners commenced apportioning it among the couple's heirs. Because some of their children were minors, a custodian or guardian was appointed. For the next several years, George Harrison served as the guardian for Anna Bland (the recipient of 190 acres), Mary Bland (who received 235 acres), and Susanna P. Bland (the owner of 200 acres). He probably was one of the late Mary B. Bland's kinsmen, for her maiden name was Harrison. William E. Bland, meanwhile, was allocated 270 acres by court decree, property called the Beaver Castle, and Theodorick Bland received 200 acres at Jordan's Point. All of the Bland heirs' parcels were devoid of structural improvements and were of equal value. The daughters' tracts were in the hands of their guardian, George Harrison, through 1874. Finally, in 1875, the 190 acres that had been attributed to Anna Bland was listed in the name of her husband, Charles Gee. The Gees' property was undeveloped.

CLOSING OUT THE NINETEENTH CENTURY

On January 23, 1875, Charles and Anna Bland Gee conveyed two tracts of land to F. P. Leavenworth and his wife of Petersburg, the acreage Anna had inherited from her father, Dr. Theodorick Bland. A plat prepared in January 1875 shows only the outline of the Gee property, an area in which archaeological work was undertaken more than a century later. At the tip of the Jordan's Point, beyond Anna Gee's boundary lines, was a lighthouse. It may have been the newly erected, square but pyramidal wooden bell tower that was built to replace the old keeper's house that was constructed in 1855 and razed in 1875 on account of shoreline erosion. A highly sensitive topographic map, prepared in 1875, reveals that approximately half of the property at Jordan's Point was cleared and half was wooded. A small clearing was near the tip of Indian Field Point and much of the Jordan's Point headlands had been cleared. A solitary structure was located to the northeast of benchmark eleven, perhaps a fishing shack or some other insubstantial building. On the tract traditionally known as the Beaver Castle were two clusters of buildings, probably associated with farming operations.

Jordan's Point and vicinity as depicted on "James River from City Point to Sloop Point," 1875, by John W. Donn. Courtesy of the National Oceanic and Atmospheric Administration.

The Jordan's Point lighthouse. Courtesy of the artist, Ed Hatch.

In 1876 William E. Bland paid taxes upon 270 acres of the 500 acre Beaver Castle tract, land that had no taxable improvements. Meanwhile, Theodorick Bland (that is, "Uncle Thee"), whose 200 acres at Jordan's Point had been credited with $300 worth of buildings during the preceding year, had increased his investment in improvements to $500. According to family tradition, he returned to Jordan's Point after the close of the Civil War, built a home on the property he had inherited from his father, and farmed for a living. His house was located on acreage that is now part of the Jordan's Point Country Club. The boundary line of Theodorick Bland's farm is shown on Anna Gee's 1875 plat.

On November 24, 1877, F. P. and Eliza C. Leavenworth deeded the tracts they had bought from the Gees to Robert Gilliam, their trustee. A deed executed in 1920 reveals that the Leavenworths' motive in conveying their land to Gilliam was to secure it from liability for any debts that Mr. Leavenworth might incur, preserving it for the support of his wife and children until the children reached adulthood. This legal maneuver is a reflection of the hard times many rural families faced after the Civil War. According to one account (perhaps written by Theodorick [Uncle Thee] Bland), the

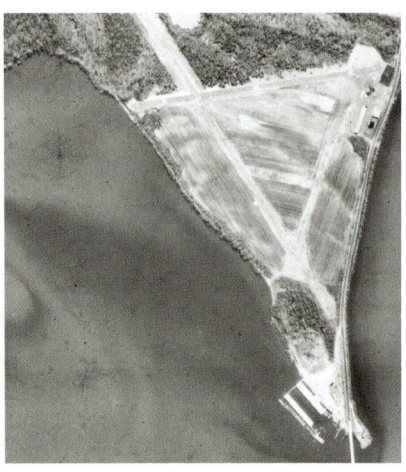

Aerial view of the Hopewell Airport, built during the late 1940s.

Leavenworths farmed their acreage and offended the Blands by cultivating part of their family cemetery, which was nearly an acre in size and irregularly shaped. A new dwelling was built at the tip of Jordan's Point in 1888, housing for the keeper of the light perched upon the bell tower erected in 1875.

On September 8, 1889, George A. and Mary S. Bland Armistead conveyed to their trustee a 40 acre tract that lay to the east of the Leavenworth couple's land. This parcel, part of the "old Jordan's Point Plantation called Jenny's that came to Mary Bland Armistead from her late father," Dr. Theodorick Bland,

The use of a backhoe to remove overburden helps archaeologists salvage cultural remains. VDHR photo.

Left: The Bland family cemetery at Jordan's Point. Courtesy of Richard Bland College. Right: The logo at the entrance to the "Jordon on the James" housing development, at Jordan's Point, uses intertwining J's to form a cipher. Photo by David K. Hazzard.

was placed in trust for the benefit of Elizabeth C. Leavenworth's children. Documents accumulated by the Bland family state that by 1893, two-fifths of the Jordan's Point farm had been sold out of the family (the Point field and the House tract) and the remainder was held by Dr. Theoderick Bland's children (Mary had "Jenny's," Sallie or Sarah had the Beaver Castle, and Theoderick had the "Middle Tract"). Thus, the site of Dr. Theoderick Bland's "shed house" was no longer in the family.

In 1929 the Leavenworth sisters sold their parents' land to the City of Hopewell. By that time erosion had taken a toll upon the tip of Jordan's Point, where a bell tower and light-keeper's house once stood. In November 1945 city officials sold the Leavenworth property to Fred (Frederick) E. and Maria Jones Hummell, who also purchased the land at the tip of the point, acreage that was owned by the Hopewell-Charles City Ferry, Inc. Then, they transferred their property to Hummell Aviation, Inc., whose officers in February 1947 conveyed the acreage back to Fred E. Hummell. In May 1955, when Mr. Hummell died, his real estate descended to his wife, Maria Jones Hummell, who retained the airport property until September 1976, when she conveyed it to J. Powell Watson. At that time, the airport tract was described as consisting of 193.8 acres. On May 19, 1986, Mr. Watson and his wife sold the 168 acre "airport property" to the Prince George Investment Company, a partnership. Its officers owned the property until it was developed into the community known as Jordan on the James.